*Law*Basics

EC LAW

THIRD EDITION

AUSTRALIA
Law Book Co.
Sydney

CANADA and USA
Carswell
Toronto

HONG KONG
Sweet & Maxwell Asia

NEW ZEALAND
Brookers
Wellington

SINGAPORE and MALAYSIA
Sweet & Maxwell Asia
Singapore and Kuala Lumpur

*Law*Basics

EC LAW

THIRD EDITION

By

Alan S. Reid, LL.B., Dip.L.P., LL.M. (Hons)

*Lecturer, Department of Law, the Robert Gordon University,
Aberdeen*

THOMSON
™
W. GREEN

First Edition published in 2002
Second Edition published in 2004

Published in 2007 by

W. Green & Son Ltd
21 Alva Street
Edinburgh EH2 4PS

www.wgreen.thomson.com

Printed in Great Britain by Athenaeum Press Ltd., Gateshead, Tyne & Wear

No natural forests were destroyed to make this product;
Only farmed timber was used and replanted

A CIP catalogue record for this book is available from the British Library

ISBN 978-0-414-01672-9

NOTE TO THIRD EDITION

This Third Edition takes into account various amendments to the EC Treaty made since the Second Edition was published. These changes include the accession of 10 Member States in May 2004 and Bulgaria and Romania in January 2007, taking the current membership of the EU to 27 Member States.

New competition rules came into force in 2004 and significant changes have occurred in the fields of free movement of persons and non-discrimination. In addition, all topics included in the Third Edition have been updated to reflect the law as of the January 1, 2007.

This edition is dedicated to the two most important girls in my life, Emma and Ellie.

Alan S. Reid   January 2007

CONTENTS

TABLE OF CASES

TABLE OF EQUIVALENCES

Previous Numbering	New Numbering
Title I	Title
Article D	Article 4
Article F	Article 6
Title II	Title II
Article G	Article 8
Title V	Title V
Article J.3	Article 13
Title VI	Title VI
Article K.7	Article 35
Part One	Part One
Article 1	Article 1
Article 2	Article 2
Article 3	Article 3
Article 3b	Article 5
Article 4	Article 7
Article 5	Article 10
Article 6	Article 12
Article 7 (repealed)	—
Part Two	Part Two
Article 8	Article 17
Article 8b	Article 19
Part Three Title I	Part Three Title I
Article 9	Article 23
Chapter I Section 1 (deleted)	Chapter 1 —
Article 12	Article 25
Article 15 (repealed)	—
Article 16 (repealed)	—
Article 18 (repealed)	—
Article 28	Article 26
Article 29	Article 27
Chapter 2	Chapter 2
Article 30	Article 28
Article 31 (repealed)	—
Article 32 (repealed)	—
Article 33 (repealed)	—
Article 34	Article 29
Article 36	Article 30
Title III Chapter 1	Title II Chapter 1
Article 48	Article 39
Article 49	Article 40
Article 50	Article 41
Article 51	Article 42

Chapter 2	Chapter 2
Article 52	Article 43
Article 53 (repealed)	—
Article 54	Article 44
Article 55	Article 45
Article 56	Article 46
Article 57	Article 47
Article 58	Article 48
Chapter 3	Chapter 3
Article 59	Article 49
Article 60	Article 50
Article 66	Article 55
Chapter 4	Chapter 4
Article 70 (repealed)	—
Title IV	Title V
Article 75	Article 71
Title V	Title VI
Chapter 1	Chapter 1
Section 1	Section 1
Article 85	Article 81
Article 86	Article 82
Article 89	Article 85
Article 90	Article 86
Section 3	Section 3
Article 92	Article 87
Article 93	Article 88
Article 94	Article 89
Chapter 2	Chapter 2
Article 95	Article 90
Chapter 3	Chapter 3
Article 100	Article 94
Article 100a	Article 95
Title VI	Title VII
Chapter 1	Chapter 1
Article 103	Article 99
Chapter 2	Chapter 2
Article 107	Article 108
Article 108	Article 109
Article 108a	Article 110
Article 109	Article 111
Title VII	Title IX
Article 115	Article 134
Title VIII	Title XI
Chapter 1	Chapter 1
Article 117	Article 136
Article 118	Article 137
Article 118a	Article 138
Article 118b	Article 139
Article 119	Article 141
Article 120	Article 143
Article 121	Article 144
Article 122	Article 145

Chapter 3	Chapter 3
Article 127	Article 150
Title XIII	Title XVI
Article 130	Article 157
Title XIV	Title XVII
Article 130a	Article 158
Title XVI	Title XIX
Article 130r	Article 174
Article 130s	Article 175
Article 130t	Article 176
Part 5	Part 5
Title I	Title I
Chapter 1	Chapter 1
Section 1	Section 1
Article 137	Article 189
Article 138	Article 190
Article 142	Article 199
Section 2	Section 2
Article 145	Article 202
Article 146	Article 203
Article 148	Article 205
Article 151	Article 207
Section 3	Section 3
Article 155	Article 211
Article 157	Article 213
Article 158	Article 214
Section 4	Section 4
Article 164	Article 220
Article 166	Article 222
Article 167	Article 223
Article 168a	Article 225
Article 169	Article 226
Article 170	Article 227
Article 171	Article 228
Article 173	Article 230
Article 174	Article 231
Article 175	Article 232
Article 176	Article 233
Article 177	Article 234
Article 182	Article 239
Article 184	Article 241
Article 186	Article 243
Article 188	Article 245
Section 5	Section 5
Article 188a	Article 246
Article 188b	Article 247
Article 188c	Article 248

Chapter 2	Chapter 2
Article 189	Article 249
Article 189a	Article 250
Article 189b	Article 251
Article 189c	Article 252
Article 190	Article 253
Article 191	Article 254

1. INTRODUCTION

Students of European law face a daunting prospect. They are essentially studying an "alien" law, since the law of the European Union stems from a supranational legal and political system far removed from the comforting familiarity of domestic law. To a certain extent, students of EC law have to unlearn what they have been taught in other law classes. Upon studying EC law, students quickly realise that cherished and long-established constitutional principles such as Parliamentary Supremacy and Parliamentary Sovereignty have to cede to the European Union concept of the rule of law.

The law of the European Union is unique. It has the power to override inconsistent domestic law and it can be used as both a shield and as a sword in domestic legal proceedings. EC law is designed to be practical and effective, even if at times it does not seem like it.

Terminology is a further complicating issue. What exactly is EC law about? Is it about the law of the individual Member States that make up the European Union? Is it about the law of the European Union or the law of the European Community? The term "European Communities" refers to the European Coal and Steel Community (ECSC) established in 1952 the European Atomic Energy Community (Euratom) and the European Economic Community (EEC) both established in 1958. These were set up among the six founding Member States. When referring to "the Community" it is this latter Community, the EEC, which is generally meant. This is why "Community" in the singular is mostly used. To complicate matters, the Treaty on European Union ("the Maastricht Treaty") in 1992 changed the name "European Economic Community" into "European Community" (EC). The contents of this study guide concern those areas of law and policy dealt with by the European Community.

The European Union, by contrast, was established among the (by then) twelve Member States by the Treaty on European Union (TEU) and marked "a new stage in the process of creating an ever closer union among the peoples of Europe". It did not replace "the European Community" which remains a separate entity within the European Union. The TEU added new fields of activity and processes to the original Treaties setting up the three Communities (above). The European Union is founded on three elements, or "pillars":

- The European Community;
- A Common Foreign and Security Policy; and
- Police and Judicial Co-operation in Criminal Matters.

This study guide restricts itself to the law of the European Community. Nevertheless, it is important to note that further deepening of European cooperation and a widening of the EU's geography is work-in-progress. Indeed, the road to full European integration still lies ahead.

1

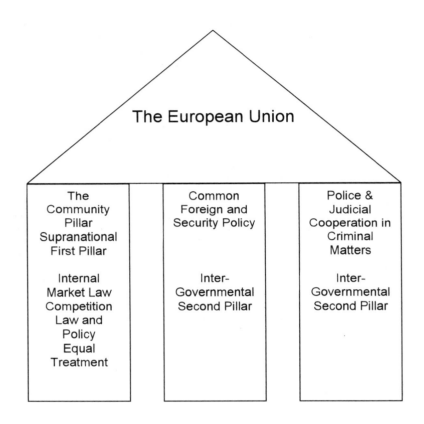

2. FROM COMMUNITY TO UNION

The establishment and development of the European Community took place against the backdrop of conflict between European nation states. Incessant warfare had resulted in such devastation that by the late 1940s it was clear that it was no longer possible for nation states, particularly those European powers who still ruled over large colonial empires, to operate political and economic policies which did not involve their immediate neighbours. At the same time, apprehension over the ambitions of the Soviet Union which by that time had occupied the Eastern part of Europe impelled the democratic states of Western Europe and the United States of America to join in the North Atlantic Treaty Organisation (NATO).

Although reconstruction of post-war Europe was under way by the end of the decade, aided in no small part by millions of dollars poured into Western Europe by the United States by way of grants and loans under the Marshall Plan, the threat of Soviet expansion prompted moves towards the creation of some form of mutual interdependence. The French statesmen, Jean Monnet and Robert Schuman devised a plan for a partnership between France and Germany for the production of coal and steel within the framework of an organisation open to the participation of the other countries of Europe. The Schuman Declaration was adopted on May 9, 1950 (a day now celebrated within the Member States as "Europe Day"). In 1951 the Treaty of Paris was signed, bringing a European Coal and Steel Community (the "ECSC") into being in April 1952. It was anticipated that not only would this pooling of the entire European coal and steel production under an independent authority eliminate the potential for conflict between France and Germany but would provide a sound basis for economic unification and expansion in the future.

The founders of the ECSC used the word "supranational" in the original Treaty to describe this independent authority. Although the Community had been created through an international treaty concluded between sovereign nations, the signatories were aware that they had created something very different from simply another international organisation. Not only did they accept mutual obligations, but they limited their own sovereign rights, transferring some of them to independent institutions over which they had no direct control and conferred on these institutions powers which they themselves did not possess. A legal system had been created to which the words "international" and "national" did not apply. The term "supranational" indicated that difference.

The European Coal and Steel Treaty then set up four institutions. These were based not on a rigid separation of powers, but on a community of interests. These institutions were:

- A High Authority formed by independent appointees of the Member States' governments, with responsibility for taking legally binding decisions and running the new Community. This body would act in the Community interest;

- A Council of Ministers made up of one representative from each of the Member States to represent the interests of those Member States (the signatories to the Treaty);
- An Assembly with delegates appointed by their respective nations' parliaments to represent the interests of the peoples of Europe; and
- A Court of Justice which would adjudicate on disputes and review the legality of the acts of the High Authority.

The signing of the European Coal and Steel Treaty in Paris on April 18, 1951 by the six founding countries (France, Germany, Italy, Belgium, Netherlands and Luxembourg) may be regarded as a first step towards European integration. Subsequently a European Atomic Power Community (Euratom) was created by the Treaty of Rome signed on March 25, 1957. The intention was to create a specialist market for atomic energy, distribute it throughout the six countries who had signed the ECSC and sell on surpluses to non-Member States. Euratom shared the Assembly and Court of Justice with the ECSC but had its own Commission (similar in nature and functions to the ECSC's High Authority).

In 1956, "The Six" had also begun negotiations to set up another Community dealing with a wider range of economic matters. A second Rome Treaty signed on the same date as the Euratom Treaty brought the new Community into effect in 1958. It was entitled "The European Economic Community" (EEC). Its whole raison d'être was to establish and ensure the effective functioning of a Common Market based on free and fair competition and the abolition of trade barriers and as its preamble stated, "to lay the foundations of an ever closer union among the peoples of Europe". While the EEC had its own separate Commission and Council of Ministers it shared the Assembly and Court of Justice with Euratom and the ECSC.

In contrast to the other two treaties, which as "traités loi" specified the exact powers of the institutions, the EEC Treaty was a "traité cadre", a framework Treaty setting out general principles, leaving it to the institutions to work out policy and the detailed measures necessary to implement such policy. The initial steps towards achieving the goal of an efficient and effective Common Market involved the establishment of a customs union eliminating all customs duties and quotas between Member States and the creation of a common customs tariff for goods arriving from other non-Member States.

The aspirations of the founders were quite clear. They included:

- The formation of a supranational organisation;
- The creation and maintenance of a tariff-free market; and
- The development of a programme which would lead to the removal of all other national economic barriers throughout Europe, sector by sector, leading to deeper economic integration and one from which it would only be a short step to eventual political union.

The Customs Union became fully operational by 1968. This meant that tariff and quota restrictions to trading between Member States had by then been abolished and that the replacement of national external tariffs by a common external tariff had been completed. However, by 1969 full freedom of movement had not yet been achieved in the markets for goods, persons, services and capital. Nor were the Community's institutions as effective as had been envisaged; decision making and legislation were taking place all too slowly. Throughout the 1970s there was pessimism about the future of the EEC. Economic crises on a global scale as well as internal political difficulties within the Member States of the Community had weakened the resolve of its members to press on with further integration.

In 1985 several crucial events occurred which added impetus to the integration process. On January 1, Jacques Delors was appointed as the new President of the European Commission. With his encouragement, the UK Commissioner (Lord Cockfield) produced a detailed White Paper on the internal market which set the date of 1992 for elimination of the remaining barriers to trade. As the European Community could only act within the limits of the powers conferred upon it by the Treaties (which the Member States had signed and ratified) further modifications to its powers could only come about through amendment to these Treaties by way of Intergovernmental Conferences (IGCs) of the Member States. Despite opposition from some Member States, an IGC took place, the outcome of which was the Single European Act of 1986. This Treaty, ratified by all Member States' was the single most important amendment to date of the EEC. It was comprised of two parts relating to its internal and external components. Its main features were to speed up the creation of a European economic market without internal frontiers and to reform all the main institutions of the Community to make them more effective, efficient and democratically accountable. This was to be achieved by:

- Inauguration of the internal market programme which was to be completed by December 31, 1992;
- Replacement of unanimity by qualified majority voting within the Council of Ministers for two-thirds of the 300 measures identified in the Cockfield White Paper as necessary to complete the internal market;
- Creation of a co-operation procedure allowing the European Parliament enhanced participation in the legislative process by giving it a second reading of proposals;
- Formalisation of the European Council (previously known as Summit Meetings between Heads of State and Government) as an organ of the European Community with increased policy-making authority;
- Recognition of the Assembly as the European Parliament;
- Creation of the Court of First Instance to ease the workload of the European Court of Justice;
- Co-operation in an economic and monetary policy;
- Common policy for research and technological development, and environment protection; and
- Harmonisation in the areas of health, safety, consumer protection, professional and vocational qualifications, public procurement, VAT and excise duties, and frontier controls.

The second part of the Single European Act contained provisions for European Political Co-operation—that is, foreign policy co-operation between governments. The Act rekindled enthusiasm for integration within Europe and acted as a stimulus to accelerate further integration.

As a result of this renewed enthusiasm for integration, an ambitious IGC was convened and on February 7, 1992 the Treaty on European Union was signed by the 12 Member States. It brought into being a new legal entity—the European Union. Of the three pillars of the European Union created by the Treaty, the first and—for our purposes—most important, was the European Communities pillar. This was composed of the three Communities which were established in the 1950s; the European Economic Community (EEC), the European Coal and Steel Community (ECSC) and Euratom. The other two pillars related to a Common Foreign and Security Policy (covering the political aspects of foreign policy as opposed to the economic aspects which are still within the Community pillar) and Justice and Home Affairs (now, since the Treaty of Amsterdam in 1997, called Police and Judicial Co-operation in Criminal Matters). These latter two pillars involve intergovernmental co-operation only.

As well as setting out a framework for the respective competences of the component parts of the Union, one of the central tenets of the Treaty was to set out detailed provisions for the organisation of Economic and Monetary Union (EMU) and a timetable for its realisation.

Modifications were also made to the EEC Treaty (which was renamed the EC Treaty) to amplify Community powers in some areas, attack what was widely perceived as a democratic deficit, strengthen the powers of the institutions and redress what appeared to be a widening gulf between the Community and its citizens.

The Treaty on European Union:

- Set out a common institutional framework for all three pillars of the Union;
- Introduced the principle of subsidiarity to its law-making process;
- Created the status of Citizen of the European Union;
- Introduced new, modified and expanded powers in the areas of economic and social cohesion (aid to less well-off regions), environmental protection, research and technological development, consumer protection, vocational training, the establishment and development of trans-European transport networks, public health protection, culture and development co-operation;
- Changed the rules on the appointment of the Commission;
- Introduced a third reading stage for the European Parliament by way of a new co-decision procedure and extensions of the previous procedures;
- Created the position of Ombudsman;
- Introduced enhanced participation in European affairs by a Committee of the Regions; and
- Created sanctions in the form of fines and/or periodic payments which could be levied by the Court of Justice in the event of a Member State failing to comply with its Community obligations.

The law contained in the (amended) EC Treaty within the Community pillar is still referred to as EC law or Community law.

After complex negotiations during its passage and some considerable delay in ratifying it within the Member States thereafter, the Treaty on European Union entered into force in November 1993.

The reforms agreed at Maastricht were widely perceived as disappointing and disillusionment with Europe was increasingly reflected in public opinion. In particular, the unity of the Community system seemed to be under attack from two quarters. Firstly, the expansion of European competences, although welcome, was achieved through intergovernmental co-operation in the second and third pillars and not through use of the supranational first pillar, thus undermining the entire ethos of European integration. Secondly, the provisions on flexibility which permitted some Member States to participate in certain policies whilst others lagged behind or opted-out entirely, undermined European unity and threatened the creation of a two-tier Europe. Examples of this were the UK opt-out from the Social Policy chapter and the UK and Danish option on membership of Economic and Monetary Union. Accordingly the issues involved were quickly revisited and in 1996 a further IGC was convened with the aim of "ensuring the effectiveness of the mechanisms and the institutions of the Community". To some extent, progress was made:

- Some matters relating to visas, asylum, immigration and other policies relating to the free movement of persons were to be incorporated into the Community pillar instead of being located in the third pillar where they were subject only to intergovernmental co-operation procedures;
- The third pillar was renamed Police and Judicial Co-operation in Criminal Matters;
- An agreement on institutional reform to provide for enlargement did not materialise. Instead, the main points agreed were that Parliament's powers would be strengthened;
- Some Member States were to be provided with the means to move to closer integration between themselves in certain specified areas;
- Acts of the institutions could be reviewed by the Court of Justice to ensure their compliance with the principle of respect for human rights;
- Provision would be made for legislation to combat discrimination; and
- Political control over a Member State guilty of certain serious and persistent breaches would all be incorporated in a new treaty agreed by all existing Member States.

On May 1, 1999 the resulting Treaty of Amsterdam came into force. The existing Treaties were then amended accordingly. This involved not only altering their content, inserting new provisions and repealing old ones, but also re-numbering most of the previous provisions.

In this respect, great care is to be exercised in identifying the correct Article of the Treaty. Pre-Amsterdam legislation and case law will refer to the old numbering scheme. In such cases, the citation will read, for example Article 30 (now Article 28). In addition, the content of some Articles was repealed, expanded or otherwise changed.

One of the most important issues that Amsterdam was supposed to resolve was the institutional position after enlargement. This matter was postponed during the IGC, and surfaced only in one of the Protocols to the Treaty of Amsterdam and several Declarations. At the European Council Cologne meeting in 1999, a further IGC was called which, through the Treaty of Nice 2000, brought the following provisions into effect on February 1, 2003:

- As from January 1, 2005 the Commission shall comprise one national from each of the Member States. It originally stated that if and when the Union consists of 27 Member States, the number of Commissioners shall be less than the number of Member States. A Protocol to the Treaty, confirmed that this rule would only apply after the Commission reaches 27 Member States and will not be applied until 2009. The exact number of Commissioners in a Union of more than 27 Member States will be set by the Council of Ministers acting unanimously, chosen according to a rotation system based on the principle of equality, and will take into account demography and geography;
- The President of the Commission received increased powers concerning internal organisation of the Commission;
- Votes in the Council were re-weighted. In addition to meeting the threshold for a qualified majority vote, the Treaty stipulates that a vote in the Council will require the support of a majority of Member States and that a Member State can request verification of whether the majority vote represents at least 62 per cent of the total population of the Union;
- Extension of qualified majority voting in the Council in a number of policy fields, reducing the necessity for unanimity;
- Extension of the co-decision procedure for law-making within the Community, giving increased authority and responsibility to the European Parliament;
- An increase in size of the European Parliament to a maximum of 732 MEPs. The Parliament was elevated to the status of privileged applicant under Article 230 (*see* Chapter 7, Judicial Review). However, with the accession of Bulgaria and Romania, the number of MEPs is now 785 as per Protocol 10(4) to the EC Treaty;
- The Council of Auditors comprises one representative from each Member State;
- Membership of the Economic and Social Committee and the Committee of the Regions was limited to 350 members each;
- Within the Court of Justice there is an increased use of chambers and a redistribution of responsibilities between it and the Court of First Instance;
- Enhanced co-operation between Member States is now easier to achieve since it only requires eight Member States to undertake action; and
- Three competences were added to the powers of the Union:

  1. The establishment of Eurojust, a unit of public prosecutors to co-ordinate the fight against crime (Article 31, TEU);
  2. A provision to combat fraud on the public finances (Article 135a, EC); and
  3. Social exclusion and modernisation of social security systems was added to the objectives of social policy (Article 137, EC).

Today there are two Communities (the ECSC expired in July 2002) comprising 27 Member States, now known collectively as the European Union. These are "The Six"' who have been joined over the last 40 years through Accession Treaties by the UK, Denmark and Ireland (1973), Greece (1981), Spain and Portugal (1986), Austria, Finland and Sweden (1995), Cyprus, Czech Republic, Estonia, Hungary, Lithuania, Latvia, Malta, Poland,

Slovakia, Slovenia (2004) and Bulgaria and Romania (2007). In addition, in October 1990 German reunification took place, adding a further 18 million people. In total, the EU now comprises a population of 492 million citizens. By virtue of the Merger Treaty of 1965, the Communities share the same institutions as does the European Union under its common institutional framework. These institutions remain legally independent although their powers are derived from their respective Treaties (EC and Euratom Treaties). Since 1979, representation in the European Parliament has been by direct vote, rather than appointment from national parliaments.

Under their agreements with the European Union, applicant countries have undertaken to fulfil stringent criteria for membership, known as the "Copenhagen Criteria". These specify that the applicant country:

- Has achieved the stability of institutions guaranteeing democracy, the rule of law, respect for human rights and the protection of minorities;
- Has a functioning market economy as well as the capacity to cope with competitive pressures and forces within the union;
- Has the ability to take on the obligations of membership, including the *acquis communautaire*. This term refers to all principles, policies, laws, practices, obligations and objectives that have been decided and agreed upon since the establishment of the original Communities, whatever the form in which it was done, whether legally binding or not. In other words, it refers to the body of rules that govern the Communities in all their fields of activity; and
- Adheres to the aims of political, economic and monetary union.

At the European Council's meeting in Laeken in December 2001, it was decided to establish a Convention on the Future of Europe, with Valéry Giscard d'Estaing, a former French President as its chairperson. The Convention consisted of 113 representatives. Its main purpose was to debate the future of the Union and the adoption of a European Union Constitution, particularly:

- Simplifying the treaties—reorganising the basic provisions of the present treaties into a single treaty;
- Setting out the powers of the Union with particular emphasis on the principle of subsidiarity;
- Considering the status of the Charter of Fundamental Rights of the European Union; and
- Clarifying the role of national parliaments within the institutional structure of the Union.

However, at the Brussels meeting of the European Council in December 2003, under the Italian Presidency, consensus on the form of a final document could not be achieved. At the time of writing, 16 countries have ratified the Constitution so far, however the Constitution is unlikely to ever come into force in light of the rejection of the Constitution by French and Dutch citizens in referendums in the summer of 2005. The Commission initiated Plan D for Democracy, Dialogue and Debate in 2004. This initiative is an attempt to generate public interest and involvement in the European integration project. The German Presidency of the Council has stated that one of its main aims is to secure agreement on the Constitution in the first half of 2007.

The Constitution would have introduced the following significant changes:

- Reform of the Qualified Majority Voting System. A three-stage test would be adopted, requiring positive agreement of at least 55% of the Member States, comprising a numerical majority of 15 Member States and representing at least 65% of the European Union population. Co-decision would become the default legislative procedure and would be extended to a number of areas that are currently found within the Third Pillar. In addition, the number of legislative measures would be reduced.
- A single market in energy and commercial policy.
- Supremacy would be enshrined in the Constitution, the Charter of Fundamental Rights would become legally binding, the Union would gain legal personality and Member States would be given the right to leave the Union.
- The nature and range of competences would be clarified.
- In Foreign and Security matters, a new post of Union Minister for Foreign Affairs would be created.
- The Presidency of the Council would be reformed to create a troika of three Member States and the European Council would become an EU institution.

---

3. SOURCES OF INFORMATION

TEXTBOOKS

A.M. Arnull, A.M. Dashwood, M. Ross, M. Dougan, E. Spaventa, and D.A. Wyatt, *Wyatt & Dashwood's European Union Law* (5th edn, Sweet and Maxwell, 2006).

D. Chalmers, C. Hadjiemmanuil, G. Monti and A. Tomkins, *EU Law—Text and Materials* (CUP, 2006).

P. Craig and G. de Burca, *EU Law—Text, Cases and Materials* (3rd edn, OUP, 2003).

K. Davies, *Understanding EU Law* (3rd edn, Routledge, 2006).

N. Foster, *Foster on EU Law*, (OUP, 2006).

J. Hanlon, *European Community Law* (3rd edn, Sweet and Maxwell, 2003).

P. Craig and G. de Burca, *EU Law—Text, Cases and Materials* (3rd edn, OUP, 2003).

K. Davies, *Understanding EU Law* (3rd edn, Routledge, 2006).

N. Foster, *Foster on EU Law*, (OUP, 2006).

J. Hanlon, *European Community Law* (3rd edn, Sweet and Maxwell, 2003).

M. Horspool and M. Humphreys, *EU Law* (4th edn, OUP, 2006).

T. Kennedy, *Learning European Law* (Sweet and Maxwell, 1998).

P. Kent, *Law of the European Union* (3rd edn, Longman, 2001).

J. Steiner, L. Woods and C. Twigg-Flesner, *Textbook on EU Law* (9th edn, OUP, 2006).

E. Szyszczak and A. Cygan, *Understanding EU Law* (Sweet and Maxwell, 2005).

J. Tillotson and N. Foster, *European Union Law: Text, Cases and Materials* (4th edn, Cavendish Publishing, 2003).

S. Weatherill, *Cases and Materials on EC Law* (7th edn, OUP, 2005).

C. Vincenzi, and J. Fairhurst, *Law of the European Community* (4th edn, Pearson, 2003).

STUDY SKILL TECHNIQUES

K. Fullerton, *Legal Research Skills for Scots Lawyers* (2nd edn, W. Green & Sons, 2007).

P. Clinch, *Using a Law Library* (Blackstone Press, 2001).

S. Stein, *Law on the Web—A Guide for Students and Practitioners* (Pearson 2003).

S. I. Strong, *How to Write Law Essays and Exams* (LexisNexis, 2003).

LEGISLATION—TREATIES, MAIN REGULATIONS AND DIRECTIVES, ETC.

N. Busby and R. Smith, *Core EU Legislation* (2006/2007, Law Matters, 2006).

N. Foster, *Blackstone's EC Legislation* (17th edn, 2006/2007, OUP 2006).

JUDGMENTS OF THE EUROPEAN COURT OF JUSTICE AND THE COURT OF FIRST INSTANCE

These are reproduced in the European Court Reports (E.C.R.) and the Common Market Law Reports (C.M.L.R.).

JOURNALS

European Law Review—E.L.Rev.
Common Market Law Review—C.M.L.Rev.
European Public Law—E.P.L.
Journal of Common Market Studies—J.C.M.S.
European Competition Law Review—E.C.L.R.

INTERNET

One of the most important sources of information is the web site of the European Union (the Europa Server)—*http://europa.eu.*

This site is the gateway to all policies, legislation and institutions of the EU. It gives multilingual access to all major issues on the EU agenda: Treaties and legislation, the Official Journal, information on the rights of European citizens, press releases from the institutions, information on the Euro (€), up-to-date information on decisions, programmes or measures adopted by the EU, publications and statistics, the nearest available sources of information and case law from the European Courts of Justice.

What's New on Europa
http://europa.eu/geninfo/whatsnew.htm

RAPID: EU Press Releases
http://europa.eu/press_room/index_en.htm
EUR-Lex, access to full-text legislative information including Treaties, legislation, case law and the Official Journal.
http://eur-lex.europa.eu/

European Parliament
http://www.europarl.europa.eu/

Council of the EU
http://www.consilium.europa.eu/

European Commission
http://ec.europa.eu/

Court of Justice
http://www.curia.europa.eu/

Court of Auditors
http://www.eca.europa.eu/

European Economic and Social Committee
http://www.eesc.europa.eu/

Committee of the Regions
http://www.cor.europa.eu/

KEEPING UP TO DATE

BBC Inside Europe
http://news.bbc.co.uk/2/hi/in_depth/europe/2003/inside_europe/default.stm

BBC Europe Today
http://www.bbc.co.uk/worldservice/programmes/europetoday/index.shtml

EU Business website
http://www.eubusiness.com/

4. SOURCES OF LAW

The founding Treaties do not define the sources of Community Law. Article 220 simply states that "The Court of Justice shall ensure that in the interpretation and application of this Treaty the law is observed". However, reflecting the diversity and supranational nature of the Community legal system, the sources of law can be classified into the following four main sources.

(1) TREATIES

The two Community Treaties which are the primary source of Community law and its ultimate legal authority:

- European Community Treaty 1957 (now the EC Treaty); and
- Euratom Treaty 1957.

Other Treaties made between Member States including those amending the founding treaties and accession treaties of new Member States:

- Merger Treaty 1965;
- Budgetary Treaties 1970; 1975;
- Single European Act 1986;
- Treaty on European Union 1992 (the Maastricht Treaty);
- Treaty of Amsterdam 1997;
- Treaty of Nice 2000; and
- The Six Treaties of Accession (1972-2006).

Treaties between the Communities and non-Member States

- Treaty establishing the World Trade Organisation;
- Lomé Conventions with the African, Caribbean and Pacific (ACP) countries; and
- Europe Agreements between the European Community and applicant countries for membership of the European Union.

(2) SECONDARY LEGISLATION

This refers to the body of Community rules adopted in accordance with the founding Treaties. It has evolved over the years from the 100 Articles of the ECSC Treaty, into a vast body of law comprising thousands of regulations, Directives, decisions, agreements and other measures. These are the binding and non-binding Acts of the institutions. Each institution must act within the limits of the powers conferred upon it by Article 249 which states:

"In order to carry out their task and in accordance with the provisions of this Treaty, the European Parliament acting jointly with the Council, the Council and the Commission shall make regulations and issue Directives, take decisions, make recommendations or deliver opinions.
A regulation shall have general application. It shall be binding in its entirety and directly applicable in all Member States.

A Directive shall be binding, as to the result to be achieved, upon each Member State to which it is addressed, but shall leave to the national authorities the choice of form and methods.

A decision shall be binding in its entirety upon those to whom it is addressed.

Recommendations and opinions shall have no binding force."

Article 249 therefore sets out three types of legally binding acts:

- Regulations
- Directives
- Decisions

And two types of non-legally binding acts:

- Recommendations
- Opinions

Legislation must have a Legal Basis

Whichever form of legislation is chosen, it fulfils a specific function in the development of Community law and therefore the Treaty specifies which type of act must be adopted to achieve a particular aim of the Community. The preamble to any piece of legislation should therefore state the Article of the Treaty on which it is based. The Treaty Article chosen will set out the legislative procedure to be followed—involving voting requirements in the Council and the extent of the European Parliament's involvement in the process.

Article 253 sets out that regulations, directives and decisions all must state the reasons on which they are based and must refer to the proposals and opinions which were required by the Treaty to be obtained. The institution concerned is not allowed to specify how it would *prefer* the objective to be pursued. Its conviction must be based on objective factors, which must be amenable to judicial review. In particular, these factors must include the aim and content of the measure (*Commission v Council Re Titanium Dioxide Waste* [1991]; *Commission v Council 'Environmental Crimes'* [2005]). The measure must therefore specify in a clear and concise manner what the principal issues of fact and law are so that the reasoning which led the institution to make its choice of legal basis may be clearly understood. If an act of an institution is not sufficiently reasoned, this constitutes a ground for annulment of the measure (*see* Chapter 7, Judicial Review).

The full citation convention for secondary legislation is as follows:

- Form of legislation (regulation, directive, etc.);
- Number of the instrument and its year of adoption (regulations are cited by number then year, directives and decisions by year then number);
- Treaty from which authority for the legislation is founded;
- The institution adopting the legislation (Commission, Council);
- Date passed;
- Title; and
- Date and page number of the Official Journal in which the measure was published.

For example—Directive 2004/38/EC on the right of citizens of the Union and their family members to move and reside freely within the territory of the Member States ([2004] O.J. L158/77).

Regulations

"A regulation shall have general application. It shall be binding in its entirety and directly applicable in all Member States".

- "General application" means that a regulation applies to any number of Member States, individuals or companies;
- "Binding in its entirety" means that the whole of the regulation must be implemented;
- "Directly applicable" means that the regulation applies in all Member States without the need for further enactment;
- "In all Member States" means that the regulation must be applied in the same way and at the same time in all Member States; and
- Regulations must be published in the Official Journal in the 23 official Community languages. They enter into force on the date specified in the act, or if no date is specified, then on the twentieth day following their publication.

Directives

"A Directive shall be binding, as to the result to be achieved, upon each Member State to which it is addressed, but shall leave it to the national authorities the choice of form and methods."

- The purpose of directives is to allow the achievement of common objectives throughout the Member States;
- Directives are addressed to Member States only;
- The Member State must enact domestic legislation to comply with the directive within a set time limit;
- The form of the implementing legislation is chosen by the Member State which can choose the most appropriate method for its own legal system;
- Once they have been correctly transposed into national law, directives are binding on individuals;
- Individuals may claim compensation if a Member State fails to implement a directive within the time limit or does so incompletely or incorrectly; and
- Directives must be published in the Official Journal in the 23 official Community languages.

Decisions

"A decision shall be binding in its entirety upon those to whom it is addressed."

- "Binding in its entirety" means that the whole of the Decision must be implemented;
- A Decision is binding only upon those to whom it is addressed;

- A Decision can be addressed to a Member State or to an individual or company;
- There is no need to enact implementing legislation;
- Decisions must be notified to those to whom they are addressed and do not come into effect until that notification has been carried out;
- Decisions can be challenged before the Court of Justice by persons who claim to be directly and individually affected; and
- Decisions affecting the rights of third parties are published in the Official Journal in the 23 official Community languages.

Recommendations and Opinions

"Recommendations and opinions shall have no binding force". They are of persuasive force only.

(3) CASE LAW OF THE EUROPEAN COURT OF JUSTICE AND THE COURT OF FIRST INSTANCE

The decisions of the Court of Justice are authoritative on all aspects of the Treaties, acts of the institutions and acts of the Member States which arise in conformity with their Treaty obligations. Unlike the common law tradition of Anglo-American systems, the civilian nature of Community law based on Continental legal systems does not rely on the doctrine of precedent and means that the Court of Justice is not rigidly bound by its own previous decisions. It may therefore depart from them if it feels the need to adapt or update its case law (*Keck and Mithouard* [1993]).

(4) GENERAL PRINCIPLES OF LAW

As well as the Treaties, the Court of Justice draws on general principles of law derived from the legal traditions of the Member States. These general principles can be used by all courts to interpret Community law. They are generally recognised as comprising:

- Proportionality—legislative measures should not go beyond what is necessary to achieve the desired objective (*Bela-Mühle v Grows Farm* [1977]);
- Legal certainty—comprising respect for legitimate expectations and the principle that European Community measures should not have retroactive effect (*Council v European Parliament* [1986]);
- Legitimate expectation (*Mulder v Minister van Landbouw en Visserij* [1988]);
- Legal professional privilege—written communication between independent (not in-house) lawyers and clients are respected (*A M & S Europe Limited v Commission* [1982]); and
- Fundamental human rights—in *Nold v Commission* [1974] the Court stated that while it was inspired by the constitutional traditions common to the Member States, it added "international treaties for the protection

of human rights" which was clearly a reference to the European Convention for the Protection of Human Rights and Fundamental Freedoms.

5. INSTITUTIONS

Although the three European Communities (ECSC, Euratom and EEC) were originally endowed with their own separate institutions, modifications over the years meant that by the early 1990's a single institutional framework was in place, serving all three Communities. The nature of these institutions is unique not only in their structure but in the way they interact in the performance of the legislative, executive and judicial functions of the Community.

There are five main institutions:

- European Commission (formerly known as the High Authority) which acts in the interests of the Community;
- Council of the European Union (formerly known as the Council of Ministers) representing the Member States;
- European Parliament (formerly known as the Assembly) representing the peoples of Europe;
- Court of Justice (to which in 1986 was added a Court of First Instance); and
- Court of Auditors (became an institution by virtue of the Maastricht Treaty).

What distinguishes an institution from any other Community body is that an institution may take binding decisions and that their members are either elected nationally (as in the case of the Council and the European Parliament) or appointed by the governments of the Member States or by the Council. Other bodies such as the Committee of the Regions either play a purely consultative role or take decisions which are not binding.

The supreme political authority of the Community, formulating and directing policy initiatives is:

- The European Council.

A number of other bodies have been created, to assist and advise the institutions. These include:

- The Economic and Social Committee—an advisory committee comprised of no more than 350 representatives of various economic and social groups such as "producers, farmers, carriers, workers, dealers, craftsmen, professional occupations, consumers and the general public". Currently there are 344 members (Articles 257 to 262).
- The Committee of the Regions—a consultative committee limited to 350 members of local and regional authorities holding an electoral mandate to represent citizens at a local level. Currently there are 344 members. The Committee advises on matters of particular concern to European

regions. In particular, the Treaty provides for it to be consulted in the
areas of culture, public health, economic and social cohesion and
environmental policy (Articles 263 and 264).
- The European Investment Bank—set up to manage the Structural Fund
  and other Community funds on a non-profit-making basis to aid the less
  developed regions and to assist in funding projects affecting more than
  one Member State where they cannot be funded sufficiently from within
  those Member States themselves (Articles 266 and 267).
- The European Central Bank and the European System of Central Banks.
  The European Central Bank is tasked with ensuring the smooth
  operation of the Euro (€), the EU currency. The European System of
  Central Banks is the umbrella term for the economic coordination and
  cooperation which takes place between the ECB and the National
  Central Banks (NCB) of the Member States, including the national
  banks of Member States that have yet to adopt the Euro.

THE EUROPEAN COMMISSION

Composition

The Commission is composed of 27 Commissioners, one for each Member
State. The Treaty of Nice stated that if and when the Union consisted of 27
Member States, the number of Commissioners would have to be less than the
number of Member States, with the exact number and nationality to be
agreed by the Council of Ministers acting unanimously and based on the
principles of equality, demography and geography. Subsequently, the failure
to ratify the European Constitution and the enlargement of the EU created a
situation whereby the Council simply decided to continue with the present
system of one Commission member for each Member State until 2009.

The method by which the Commission is appointed is that after
consulting the European Parliament, the Member States first nominate the
President of the Commission by qualified majority. Thereafter, in
consultation with the President they nominate individual Commissioners for
a renewable five-year term who are chosen on grounds of their general
competence and "whose independence is beyond doubt". The Commission as
a body is then subject to a vote of approval by the European Parliament. The
Parliament may not choose which of the Commissioners it likes (or dislikes).
Approval is by a vote of confidence en bloc. After approval by the
Parliament, they are appointed by the governments of the respective Member
States.

The Commission is subject to other supervision by the Parliament, as
follows:

- Parliament may censure the Commission;
- Parliament must receive monthly reports from the Commission on the
  implementation of the budget; and
- Parliament must be presented with the Commission's Annual General
  Report.

To ensure their independence Commissioners are forbidden to seek or take
instructions from any government or other body and must refrain from any
action which is not compatible with their duties. All the Member States have

accepted this principle and no influence is brought to bear upon the Commissioners in the performance of their tasks. Their duties are solely to further the wider interests of the Community. During their term of office, Commissioners may not engage in any other occupation and even after they retire, they are bound to behave with integrity and discretion as regards the acceptance of certain appointments or benefits.

A Commissioner will be forced to resign if the President requests such resignation, having first of all obtained the collective approval of the Commission.

As well as allowing Commissioners to fulfil their tasks with complete impartiality, the collegiate nature of the Commission also protects them from undue pressure. Commissioners do not fulfil individual roles under the Treaty. Decisions are thus made by simple majority, dissenting opinions are not published and all members of the college of Commissioners bear collective responsibility on the political level for all decisions adopted.

Functions and Powers

The administrative responsibility of the Commission is divided up into 26 Directorates-General, at least one of which is allocated by the President to the portfolio of an individual Commissioner. They cover such specific areas of responsibility such as external relations (DGI), competition (DGIV), and so on. Each Commissioner is assisted by a cabinet headed by a Chef de Cabinet. There are also specialised services such as the Legal Service which advises the Directorates-General and represent the Commission in legal proceedings, and the Statistical and Publications Office. The total staff of the Commission is approximately 25,000 and comprises administrative and secretarial support staff, experts, translators and interpreters.

The Commission's powers and functions are laid down in the Treaty under Articles 211 to 219. They fall into three main categories.

(1) *Guardian of the Treaties*

The Commission has been given the power to ensure that the provisions of the Treaty and the measures adopted for their implementation are applied.

It monitors the performance of the Member States in complying with their Treaty obligations and may receive complaints from individuals or companies who believe that a Member State is infringing their Community rights. Under Article 226 proceedings, the Commission may investigate and prosecute Member States alleged to be in breach of their Treaty obligations (*Commission v United Kingdom 'Electrical Works'* [2007]).

These obligations (sometimes known as "the loyalty clause" of the Treaty) are set out in Article 10 which states that:

"Member States must take all appropriate measures, whether general or particular, to ensure fulfilment of the obligations arising out of this Treaty or resulting from action taken by the institutions of the Community. They shall facilitate the achievement of the Community's tasks. They shall abstain from any measure which could jeopardise the attainment of the objectives of this Treaty".

When the Commission considers that a Member State has not fulfilled an obligation under Community law, it takes the following steps:

- It reminds the government in question of its obligations and invites it to take the necessary measures or submit its observations, all within a time limit set by the Commission, normally two months;
- If no action is taken by the Member State and no observations are received, or if those that were submitted do not convince the Commission, it delivers a "reasoned opinion" on the matter and lays down a time limit within which the Member State must comply;
- If the Member State does not comply, the Commission may bring the matter before the Court of Justice; and
- If the Court finds that the Member State has indeed failed to fulfil its obligation, "the State shall be required to take the necessary steps to comply with the judgment".

The procedure for enforcing Member States' fulfilment of their Community obligations is therefore in two stages. The first is an informal stage during which the Commission issues the formal notice and eventually a reasoned opinion to the Member State. In practice though, the Commission endeavours to negotiate a settlement. The second stage is the formal judicial stage where the Commission refers the Member State to the Court of Justice.

There is also a right for a Member State to take action against another Member State under Article 227 for failure to fulfil its Community obligations. The procedure requires that the matter be brought to the attention of the Commission. Proceedings then mirror those under Article 226, with the added requirement that the Commission requests the observations of *both* Member States involved. Actions brought under this heading are extremely rare as this procedure tends to be politically contentious. To date, only two cases have reached the Court, *France v UK* [1979] and *Belgium v Spain* [2000].

Since 1993, Article 228(2) of the Treaty provides that in cases where the Member State has not taken the necessary steps to comply with the judgment of the Court, it shall, after giving the Member State the opportunity to submit its observations, issue a reasoned opinion specifying the points on which the Member State has not complied and fixing a time limit for this to be carried out. In case of non-compliance, the Commission may bring the matter again to the Court and specify the amount of the lump sum or penalty payment to be paid. If the Court finds that the Member State has indeed not complied with its judgment, it may impose a lump sum or penalty payment (*Commission v Greece* [2000]). As well as the penalties provided for in the Treaty to encourage Member States to fulfil their Community obligations, pecuniary sanctions can also be imposed on Member States where they breach Community law to the detriment of an individual (*see* Member State Liability).

The Commission also monitors the acts of the Council, the Parliament and the European Central Bank and may initiate an action against them when it is believed that:

- Their failure to act constitutes an infringement of the Treaty (Article 232); or

- An act of the institution constitutes an infringement of the Treaty (Article 230).

(2) *Initiator of Community Action*

The Commission has historically had the right of legislative initiative in that it is empowered to propose legislation for its adoption by the Council and the European Parliament acting in accordance with the Community's legislative procedures. Legislation must encompass three core objectives. First, the Commission must identify the European interest; secondly, it must organise consultation as widely as necessary and thirdly, it must respect the principle of subsidiarity (*see* Chapter 6, European Law and National Law). In fulfilment of this task, the Commission works closely with the Union's two consultative bodies, the Economic and Social Committee and the Committee of the Regions, and consults them on most items of draft legislation.

The Treaty on European Union now allows the Council and Parliament to request that the Commission submit appropriate proposals for legislation where these are required for the purpose of implementing the Treaty.

The Commission will then issue preparatory documents such as Green Papers containing a description of a problem and its proposal for solving it; this will be followed by a White Paper outlining the proposed legislation for consultation. The general principle of transparency that the public should have the widest possible access to documents held by the Commission, the Parliament and the Council—subject to public interest or the rights of privacy of the individual—has been adopted through Regulation 1049/2001 which sets out that refusal to grant access must be based on one of the exceptions provided for within the regulation and must be justified on the grounds that disclosure of the document in question would be harmful.

The Commission's significant role in shaping the Community's priorities has increased in importance over recent years—for example in preparing for the completion of the single market and for enlargement of the Union in the twenty-first century. In July 2001, the Commission also initiated a wide-ranging debate throughout the Member States by publishing a major White Paper on the Reform of European Governance, paving the way for the Convention on the Future of Europe.

(3) *Executive of the Community*

The Commission has been given its own power of decision which it exercises in the functioning and development of the common market, for example in furtherance of the Community's competition policy where it administers and enforces the competition rules, and regulates mergers, joint ventures and acquisitions.

It also administers the customs union, the common agricultural policy, state aids and the common commercial policy. Although the majority of European policies are administered by the Member States themselves the Commission has significant supervisory powers. In this connection it may make regulations which must be observed within the Member States and ensures that these regulations are carried out.

A significant part of its executive function is to manage the Community budget for submission to the Council and administer special funds such as the European Agricultural Guidance and Guarantee Fund, the European

Regional Development Fund, the Cohesion Fund and the European Social Fund which all form part of the budget.

Under the Euratom Treaty, the Commission has also been given the power to borrow on the world financial markets and to loan money for the financing of atomic energy projects. It also finances infrastructure and industrial projects. The borrowing is carried out by the Commission but the administration of the resources thus acquired is carried out by the European Investment Bank.

The Commission also acts as negotiator of international trade and co-operation agreements with third countries, or groups of countries, which the Council then concludes.

The Commission can also act by way of delegated legislative power from the Council, known as "Comitology". This practice of decision-making involves the Commission's legislative activities being supervised by the Council under a complex system involving the submission of the Commission's draft implementing measures to committees composed of officials from Member States.

The European institutional structure is not characterised by a rigid separation of powers. The Commission for example plays a role that is legislative, executive, judicial and administrative. It is:

- The guardian of the Treaties;
- Initiator and co-ordinator of Community policy; and
- The executive agency of the Community.

COUNCIL OF THE EUROPEAN UNION ("THE COUNCIL")

The Council—also referred to as the Council of Ministers—is a body with the characteristics of both a supranational and an intergovernmental organisation. That is to say, it acts as a major player in Community decision-making and has a substantial role to play under the other two "pillars" of the European Union involving co-operation between the Union's Member States. It is composed of representatives from the Member States at ministerial level, authorised to commit the government of that Member State. In practice this means that its membership fluctuates depending on the subject under discussion. For example, the General Affairs Council deals with institutional and policy issues and is attended by national Foreign Ministers. Ministers for Agriculture, Transport, Finance, etc., constitute the membership of the Council when it discusses policy and legislation in those areas. In total, there are nine different Council configurations.

The Council is assisted in its work by COREPER (The Committee of Permanent Representatives) consisting of senior national ambassadors and their deputies who are permanently located in Brussels. The work of this Committee allows decisions to be made by the Council by examining Commission proposals and preparing items for discussion at Council meetings. COREPER is assisted by a range of specialist advisory committees.

(1) Under the European Community Treaty, the Council's powers and functions are laid down in Article 202 to Article 210. The Council:

- Is the European Union's main decision-making institution and final legislative authority exercising power for the whole spectrum of the Community's activities.

The Treaty on European Union strengthened the role of the European Parliament and now many of the Council's powers must be shared with Parliament. These relate not only to budgetary power (where it has always been the case), but also to the introduction of a co-decision procedure for enacting legislation. As a consequence, a wide range of legislation such as that relating to the single market, consumer affairs, trans-European networks, education and health is adopted jointly by both the Parliament and the Council.

Depending on the subject under discussion and the voting procedures specified in the Treaty, the Council acts by a simple majority of its members, by a qualified majority or by unanimous decision. Where the Council acts by a qualified majority, the votes of each of its members are weighted as follows:

Country	Votes
Austria	10
Belgium	12
Bulgaria	10
Cyprus	4
Czech Republic	12
Denmark	7
Estonia	4
Finland	7
France	29
Germany	29
Greece	12
Hungary	12
Ireland	7
Italy	29
Latvia	4
Lithuania	7
Luxembourg	4
Malta	3
Netherlands	13
Poland	27
Portugal	12
Romania	14
Spain	27
Slovakia	7
Slovenia	4
Sweden	10
United Kingdom	29
TOTAL	345

For example, if the Commission considers that a proposal on certain aspects of tackling unemployment throughout the Community is required, it may table a proposal under Title VIII (Employment) of the Treaty. Within that title, Article 129 sets out:

"The Council, acting in accordance with the procedure referred to in Article 251 and after consulting the Economic and Social Committee and the Committee of the Regions, may adopt incentive measures designed to encourage co-operation between Member States and to support their action in the field of employment through initiatives aimed at developing exchanges of information and best practices".

This means that Article 251 which sets out the co-decision procedure in detail must be used. In turn Article 251 specifies the voting procedure necessary within the Council in order to enact the legislation proposed by the Commission. In this case it is qualified majority voting.

For matters within the Community "pillar" most of the decisions are taken by qualified majority, since 43 areas of competence are now subject to the co-decision procedure, post-Nice. The areas covered by co-decision include some of the most significant policy areas such as free movement, non-discrimination on grounds of nationality and the internal market. Of the 43 areas subject to co-decision, only nine of these areas still require the Council to act unanimously. The areas subject to unanimity include taxation, industry, culture, regional and social funds and the framework programme for research and technology development.

The Treaty of Nice originally envisaged a voting system for the 25 Member States. In a Union of 27, where decisions in the Council are to be taken by way of qualified majority, the rules are as follows. Firstly, there must be at least 255 votes in favour. Secondly, a majority of the Member States must be in favour of the measure. In some cases the Treaty may require a two-thirds majority. Thirdly, a Member State can request verification that the qualified majority comprises at least 62 per cent of the total population of the Union before the act may be adopted. If the Constitutional Treaty were to enter into force, the voting scheme would be amended and simplified such that, in most cases, a qualified majority would be calculated as being 55 per cent of the Member States in favour, which would be at least 15 in number, representing 65 per cent of the Union's population.

Legislation takes the form of regulations, directives, decisions, recommendations and opinions (*see* Chapter 4, Sources of Law).

The Council may also adopt conclusions of a political nature or other types of acts such as declarations or resolutions. Furthermore, the Council establishes requirements for the Commission to exercise the implementing powers conferred upon it.

A significant criticism of the Council was that until recently, voting in the Council remained secret. The Treaty of Amsterdam however has provided for more transparency by allowing greater access to Council, Commission and European Parliament documents, subject to limits on the grounds of public and private interest (*see* above, under "The Commission").

Community legislation as well as the Council's common positions forwarded to the European Parliament are published in the Official Journal in all 23 official languages.

The Council also:

- Co-ordinates the general economic policies of the Member States (subject to the principle of subsidiarity);
- Concludes international agreements on behalf of the European Communities (which are negotiated by the Commission and require, in some cases, Parliament's consultation or assent) between the Communities and a state, a group of states or international organisations; and
- In conjunction with the European Parliament, adopts the Community budget after its preparation by the Commission.

(2) Under the Treaty on European Union and by unanimous vote—except for joint actions where qualified majority voting is the rule—the Council:

- Takes the decisions necessary to define and implement the Common Foreign and Security Policy by deciding on joint actions and common positions; and
- Co-ordinates the activities of the Member States, decides on common positions and framework decisions, draws up conventions and adopts measures under the third "pillar" of the European Union, Police and Judicial Co-operation in Criminal Matters.

The Presidency of the Council is held by each Member State on a six-monthly rotating basis and plays a vital part as the driving force in the legislative and political decision-making process. It organises and chairs all meetings and works out compromises to resolve difficulties. The Presidency, assisted by the Secretary-General of the Council who also acts as High Representative for the Common Foreign and Security Policy, also represents the Union for foreign and security matters.

THE EUROPEAN PARLIAMENT

Composition

The European Parliament presently consists of 785 members representing 492 million citizens in 27 Member States of the European Union and since 1979 has been directly elected every five years throughout all the Member States. The Treaty of Nice provided that the number of MEPs was not to exceed 732. Protocol 10(4) of the EC Treaty permits a temporary rise in the maximum membership of the Parliament as a result of the accession of the new Member States. Citizens of the European Union as well as citizens of the Union living in a Member State of which they are not nationals, are eligible to vote and stand for election.

From January 1, 2007, the allocation of seats is as follows:

Country	Seats
Austria	18
Belgium	24
Bulgaria	18
Cyprus	6
Czech Republic	24
Denmark	14
Estonia	6
Finland	14
France	78
Germany	99
Greece	24
Hungary	24
Ireland	13
Italy	78
Latvia	9
Lithuania	13
Luxembourg	6
Malta	5
Netherlands	27
Poland	54
Portugal	24
Romania	35
Slovakia	14
Slovenia	7
Spain	54
Sweden	19
United Kingdom	78
TOTAL	785

MEPs sit in nine political groups rather than in national delegations. Though its committee meetings generally take place in Brussels, it meets in plenary sitting at Strasbourg for one week a month. Parliament's secretariat is located in Luxembourg. During its sessions, simultaneous translation of its debates is provided and all documentation is translated and published in the Official Journal in the official Community languages. It elects its own president and 14 vice-presidents who together form "the Bureau"—the executive body which drafts agendas, decides on matters of competence and makes the preliminary draft of Parliament's budget.

As well as exercising its three main functions (below) Parliament takes an active part in Europe's political life by commissioning reports and passing resolutions on issues of a social and political nature such as concern for human rights. It has also contributed in no small measure to the establishment of a European Veterinary Agency in Dublin and the creation of the European Anti-Fraud Office for budgetary matters.

Functions and Powers

The functions and powers of Parliament are laid out in Articles 189 to 201. They fall into three main categories:

- Supervisory
- Legislative
- Budgetary

Supervisory
Parliament has general supervisory powers over the other institutions of which the most powerful is its ability to hold the Commission accountable for its activities.

At the request of a quarter of its members, Parliament may set up temporary Committees of Inquiry to investigate alleged contraventions or maladministration in the implementation of European law, and to appoint a Parliamentary Ombudsman to investigate complaints such as discrimination, refusal of information or needless delays on the part of other institutions (except for the Court of Justice and the Court of First Instance).

It may receive petitions from individuals or companies in the Member States on any matter within the Union's fields of activities.

Members of the European Parliament can put written or oral questions to the Commission and to the Council or make recommendations.

Legislative
Originally, the Treaty of Rome allowed the European Parliament to act only in a consultative capacity. The Treaty on European Union and the Treaty of Amsterdam have extended this purely advisory role to one which fully involves Parliament in the legislative process. In many areas the power of decision is now shared by the Council and Parliament. The extent to which this is exercised is specified within the Treaty depending on the nature of the provision authorising action by the Community for a particular purpose (the legal basis).

Normally, legislation is enacted by one of the three main procedures— co-decision, consultation or assent. There is also a fourth procedure—the co-operation procedure—allowing Parliament two readings of proposals but containing no provision for compulsory conciliation. The Treaties of Amsterdam and Nice significantly extended the scope of the co-decision procedure which means that in practice it has almost entirely replaced the co-operation procedure.

(a) Co-decision procedure
This procedure is laid down in Article 251 and enables Parliament to share decision-making power equally with the Council. A legal act is adopted if Council and Parliament agree at first reading. If they disagree, a "conciliation committee" composed of equal numbers of MEPs and members of the Council, with the Commission present, endeavours to find a compromise on which both the Council and Parliament can subsequently agree. However, if agreement does not result Parliament can reject the proposal outright by an absolute majority. The co-decision procedure applies to a wide range of issues such as the free movement of workers, consumer protection, education, culture, health and trans-European networks.

(b) Consultation procedure
The consultation procedure requires an opinion from Parliament before the Council can adopt a legislative proposal from the Commission. Neither the

Commission nor the Council is obliged to accept Parliament's amendments. Once Parliament has given its opinion, the Council can adopt the proposal without amendments or adopt it in an amended form. The consultation procedure applies to the common agricultural policy, harmonisation of indirect taxation, aspects of environmental policy and matters connected with the Economic and Monetary Union.

(c) Assent procedure
The assent procedure applies to those legislative areas in which the Council acts by unanimous decision. Since the Treaty of Amsterdam this has been limited to the organisation and objectives of the Structural and Cohesion Funds. Parliament's assent is also required for international agreements concluded between the Union and a non-member country or group of countries, such as the accession of new Member States and association agreements with third countries (absolute majority of Parliament's total membership required).

Budgetary
The European Parliament is jointly involved with the Council in the budgetary procedure from the preparation stage, notably in laying down the general guidelines and the type of spending, voting on the annual budget prepared by the Commission and overseeing its implementation (Article 272).

Its main power concerns the non-compulsory items on the budget such as social and regional policy, research and aid to Central and Eastern non-member countries. The compulsory items of the Community's budget—mainly those relating to the Common Agricultural Policy—call for a more limited input from Parliament.

THE COURTS OF JUSTICE OF THE EUROPEAN COMMUNITIES

The origins of the Court of Justice can be traced to the founding Treaties (ECSC, Euratom and the EEC) which established a Court of Justice for each Community. These have since been merged into one single Court of Justice for the European Communities. Although the Treaty refers to it as "the Court of Justice" it is also known as the European Court of Justice or the European Court. Both Community Courts (the Court of Justice and its associated Court of First Instance) are based in Luxembourg. They should not be confused with the European Court of Human Rights which has its home in Strasbourg which is *not* an institution for the European Union. It is the role of the Court of Justice to be the guardian of European Union law in accordance with Article 220 which states simply that "The Court of Justice shall ensure that in the interpretation and application of this Treaty the law is observed". The law referred to consists of the Treaties, secondary legislation (such as regulations, directives and decisions) and the case law of the Court itself. The Court of First Instance operates under Article 225.

The Court of Justice

Composition

From January 2007, the Court consists of 27 judges, one from each Member State. It may sit in plenary session, as a Grand Chamber consisting of 13 judges, or in chambers of three or five judges. Certain legal actions may require the court to sit as a full court, however the Court also has the right to decide to sit as a full court of its own motion. Member States or Community institutions party to legal proceedings may request that the court convene as a Grand Chamber and the Court also has the discretion to sit as a Grand Chamber of its own motion. Its deliberations take place in private and result in a single, collegiate judgment. The working language of the Court is French, though documents are translated into all official languages of the Community.

The Court is assisted by eight Advocates-General whose task it is to examine the cases and deliver reasoned opinions to the Court. Both judges and Advocates-General are appointed for a period of six years. The President of the Court is elected every three years by its judges, who are chosen from those:

"whose independence is beyond doubt and who possess the qualifications required for appointment to the highest judicial offices in their respective countries or who are jurisconsults of recognised competence by common accord of the governments of the Member States."

Each Member State has a judge on the Court to represent the legal tradition of that particular country rather than the Member State itself. The Court is also assisted by a Registrar, Legal Secretaries and two Directorates.

Functions and Powers

The Court's functions and powers are set out in Article 220 to Article 245 as well as within its own Rules of Procedure (most recently amended in 2005: [2005] O.J. L288/51).

The Court originally had four main areas of jurisdiction:

(1) Infringement actions against Member States, particularly—
(a) Commission v Member States (Article 226);
(b) Member State v Member State (Article 227);
(c) Member State's failure to fulfil a Treaty obligation (Article 228).

(2) Non-contractual liability of the Community (Article 288) and compensation for damage in that event (Article 235). The jurisdiction contained in Article 235 has now been transferred to the CFI.

(3) The legality of Community action or inaction (Article 230 and Article 232). This has also been transferred to the CFI.

(4) Preliminary rulings on the interpretation and validity of European law at the request of a national court or tribunal (Article 234).

In order to enforce a judgment, the Commission may bring a further infringement action against a Member State under Article 228. Since 1993, the Court has also been given the power to impose a financial penalty on a Member State if that state still refuses to comply with the Court's judgment or its Treaty obligations (Article 228(2)).

The Court also has jurisdiction to rule on:

- Disputes concerning the European Investment Bank (Article 237);
- Arbitration clauses contained in a contract concluded by or on behalf of the Community (Article 238) (now a CFI power);
- Disputes submitted under special agreements (Article 239); and
- Compatibility with the Treaties of international agreements entered into by the Community (Article 300(6)).

The Court of Justice acts both as a Court of First Instance and as an Appeal Court from the Court of First Instance.

Its procedure generally falls into four stages (though the second stage is often omitted):

- Written proceedings;
- Investigation or preparatory inquiry;
- Oral proceedings; and
- Judgment (the formal ruling of which is published in the Official Journal) and the full judgment together with the Advocate-General's opinion, is published in the European Court Reports (E.C.R.) in all Community languages.

The Court of First Instance
To ease the workload of the Court of Justice, the Single European Act provided for the creation of a new Court of First Instance. It began sitting in 1989, with limited jurisdiction—staff cases, competition and anti-dumping cases and some matters relating to the ECSC and Euratom. Since 1993 it has heard all cases brought by natural or legal persons including actions for judicial review and actions for damages against Community institutions or the Member States. The Treaty of Nice introduced a number of changes designed to streamline the workings of the Court. Changes included:

- Judicial panels with a right of appeal on points of law to the CFI. To date there are two judicial panels, namely the European Civil Service Tribunal and the Intellectual Property judicial panel.
- Jurisdiction to hear and determine at first instance actions on Judicial Review, Failure to Act, non-contractual liability of the Community, arbitration clauses and disputes concerning the European Investment Bank and national central banks (with the exception of those reserved in the Court's Statute for hearing before the Court of Justice or assigned to a judicial panel). There is a right of appeal to the Court of Justice on points of law only. In 2004, the CFI gained further jurisdiction over state aid, trade protection measures, acts of the Council where it directly exercises implementing powers and acts of the European Central Bank and the Commission (except for actions under enhanced co-operation).
- In limited instances, the Court of Justice may grant the CFI jurisdiction as regards the Article 234 preliminary ruling procedure.
- If there is a serious risk of the unity or consistency of Community law being affected, the Court of First Instance's first Advocate-General may

propose, within one month of the CFI's decision, that the Court of Justice reviews the decision of the CFI.

* The Court can establish its own Rules of Procedure. The Council approves the Rules of Procedure by way of qualified majority.

The Court of First Instance consists of one judge from each Member State appointed under the same criteria as the Judges of the Court of Justice. It may sit with one judge in chambers of three or five judges, in a Grand Chamber of 13 judges or in plenary session.

COURT OF AUDITORS

The Court of Auditors was set up in 1975 to control and supervise the implementation of the budget. It became a full institution in 1993 under the Treaty on European Union. Its main function is to scrutinise the Commission's management of the Community budget, examine its legality, regularity of revenue and expenditure and ensure its sound financial management. As an independent audit body (rather than a "court") it is also viewed by Parliament as an essential tool in establishing greater financial control and good management of the Community. On the basis of the Court of Auditors' reports, it is the European Parliament which gives the Commission final discharge for the adoption of the annual budget. It is composed of one full-time member chosen by the Council (after consulting the European Parliament) from each Member State among persons who have had relevant auditing experience and whose independence is beyond doubt.

Its powers and functions are set out in Articles 246 to 248.

THE EUROPEAN COUNCIL

As well as these institutions there is also a supreme, policy-making body known as the European Council. It should not be confused with the Council of the European Union (above) or with the Council of Europe, an international organisation concerned mainly with human rights and based in Strasbourg.

Since 1974, the informal meetings of Heads of State and Government (previously known as "summit meetings") have been formalised into biannual meetings hosted by the Member State holding the Presidency of the Union. The President of the Commission also attends these gatherings. Although the European Council possesses no formal powers and thus plays no part in the legislative machinery, its meetings provide momentum for European integration by the injection of political will at the very highest level, to promote co-ordination and clarification of inter-Community relations and set out policy initiatives. It therefore may set out general guidelines for action to be taken at Community level by the Council and the Commission. Its informal discussions also act as a forum for co-ordination of Member States' foreign policies to maximise their influence on world affairs (*see* Article 4, TEU).

The Treaty of Amsterdam introduced new powers for the European Council allowing it to determine the existence of a "serious and persistent breach by a Member State" of the principles of liberty, democracy, respect for human rights and fundamental freedoms, and the rule of law, "after inviting the government of the Member State in question to submit its observations" (Article 7).

The Presidency of the European Council is held by the Member State holding the six-monthly Presidency of the Council of the European Union.

Accompanied by ever-increasing media attention, the European Council continues to provide a significant focus of authority and leadership for Europe. If the Constitution had entered into force, the European Council would have become an institution of the EU in its own right and would be represented by a President, with a term of office of two and a half years.

---

6. EUROPEAN LAW AND NATIONAL LAW

DIRECT EFFECT

The three European Communities were set up through an international treaty. International treaties are agreements between states affecting relations between them and do not create rights for citizens. However, the Community legal order differs in that it does create rights within Member States for the nationals of those states, as individuals. Certain provisions of Community law create enforceable private rights for citizens which may be exercised through national courts as if they were part of the law of the land. This individual right is known as "direct effect" and means that individuals can pursue their Community rights through their own local courts. Direct effect was not set out in the founding Treaties, but was developed through the case law of the Court of Justice.

Direct Effect of Treaty Articles

The leading case is that of *Van Gend en Loos NV v Nederlandse Administratie der Belastingen* [1963]. Van Gend en Loos, a Dutch transport company, imported chemicals from Germany on which it was charged customs duty of eight per cent of the value of the goods. The company challenged this on the grounds that when the EEC Treaty came into effect in the Netherlands, the duty was only three per cent and Article 12 of the Treaty required Member States to refrain from introducing any new customs duties on imports and exports of goods—a negative obligation. The Dutch Customs Authorities argued that the Treaty did not allow an individual the right to bring an action on the grounds of infringement of the Treaty. The Court of Justice disagreed and stated that it was necessary to examine the spirit, general scheme and wording of the provision in question. It stated that the EEC Treaty was more than an international agreement which created obligations between states only. It had established a common market and institutions which had been given powers to legislate not only for its Member States but also for individuals. It continued:

> "the Community constitutes a new legal order of international law for the benefit of which the states have limited their sovereign rights, albeit within limited fields and the subjects of which comprise not only

Member States but also their nationals. Independently of the legislation of the Member States, Community law therefore not only imposes obligations on individuals but is also intended to confer on them rights which become part of their legal heritage.

The Court then set out the criteria for direct effect to be applicable. For an individual to rely on a provision of European law within a national court, the provision in question:

- Must be clear and unambiguous in its terms;
- Must be unconditional, that is, not subject to any qualifications; and
- Must take effect without any further implementing or discretionary measures either by Member States or by Community institutions.

Van Gend en Loos was soon followed by a number of other similar cases challenging Member States' fulfilment of their Treaty obligations, both negative (refraining from acting in a certain way) and positive (requiring to carry out an action (*Lütticke* [1971])). In such cases, individuals and the state are in a vertical relationship—the state at the apex and the individual beneath, allowing an individual the right to sue a Member State within his own national court when he considers that it has not complied with its Community obligations.

Member State

Individuals

Horizontal as well as Vertical Direct Effect?

"Horizontal direct effect" on the other hand, is a relationship between equals—one individual or company—whereby each can sue one another within a national court to assert rights under European law.

Member State

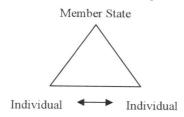

Individual ⟷ Individual

In the case of *Defrenne v SABENA* [1976], Ms Defrenne, an air hostess working for the Belgian airline, challenged her employer's policy of compulsorily retiring its female cabin crew, but not its male crew, at the age of 40. Ms Defrenne alleged that this was contrary to Article 119 (now Article 141) covering equal pay. Based on the *Van Gend en Loos* criteria, the Court of Justice stated the provisions of Article 119 produced horizontal direct effect and conferred on Ms Defrenne a right to pursue her Community rights under the Treaty against her employer.

Thus if a Treaty Article satisfies the three criteria set out in the *Van Gend en Loos* case it will produce direct effect—vertical and horizontal—and may be relied upon by individuals. Through the continuing jurisprudence of the Court, Treaty Articles concerning the free movement of goods, persons, equal pay and competition now possess the character of direct effect and allow individuals to pursue their Community rights through their own national courts.

Direct Effect of Regulations

Regulations generally apply directly within Member States without any implementing measures. Article 249 states that "a regulation ... shall be ... directly applicable in all Member States". Direct applicability, however, does not necessarily mean that regulations are directly effective. They still have to satisfy the *Van Gend en Loos* criteria before this is so (*Marimex* [1972]). All that direct applicability means is that there is no need for further legislation to be enacted by Member States incorporating the provision into national law. A regulation becomes law when it is published in the Official Journal.

Direct Effect of Decisions

Article 249 sets out a decision as being "binding in its entirety upon those to whom it is addressed". In practice a decision can be addressed to one or more Member States or one or more individuals. If a decision which is addressed to a Member State fulfils the *Van Gend en Loos* criteria it can also possess direct effect and give rights to individuals (*Grad* [1970]).

Direct Effect of Directives

It must be stressed at this juncture that directives are never directly applicable and were never designed to be. Article 249 states that "a directive shall be binding as to the result to be achieved" but that the choice of "form and methods" is left to the Member State. Directives thus always require some enacting measure to be carried out and may entail a wide measure of discretion on the part of the Member State. Nevertheless, under certain conditions directives may be directly effective, on the basis that failure to implement a directive is a failure to grant citizens of a Member State their rights under the EC Treaty. Such inaction is discriminatory, a violation of Article 10 of the EC Treaty and offends against the principle of personal bar/estoppel. In the case of *Grad*, as the time limit for implementation had expired, the provisions of the directive in question requiring Member States to amend their VAT systems could produce direct effect.

In the case of *Van Duyn v Home Office* [1974], the Court examined the wording, nature and general scheme of Directive 64/221 on which Ms Van Duyn relied and stated that a clear and precise obligation had been set out which was not subject to the adoption of subsequent acts on the part either of the Community or of Member States. Finally, the directive imposed a specific limitation on the discretion of the Member State in the field of public security. Ms Van Duyn's challenge to the Member State (the UK) was allowed by the Court because the effectiveness (*effet utile*) of the directive would be weakened if individuals were unable to enforce rights conferred on them through the courts. However, it should be noted that direct effect of directives may be relied upon only:

- After the expiry of the time allowed for its implementation into national law by the Member State (*Ratti* [1978]);
- If the Directive satisfies the three criteria of *Van Gend en Loos*; and
- Where the Member State has not implemented the directive or has incorrectly or incompletely transposed the terms of the directive into national law (*Becker* [1982]; *Emmot* [1990]).

Horizontal as well as Vertical Direct Effect for Directives?

In *Marshall v Southampton Area Health Authority* [1986] the Court had to ascertain whether Directive 79/7 could be relied upon not only against the state but also against another individual or company, as in the *Defrenne* case; in other words, whether directives could be said to have horizontal as well as vertical direct effect. Miss Marshall had sued her employer whose policy compelled women to retire at 60, five years earlier than male retirement age. The Court of Justice was asked to rule on whether the directive had direct effect and if so, whether this could be horizontal as well as vertical. The Court pointed out that directives are only binding on the Member State to whom they addressed and that therefore "a Directive may not of itself, impose obligations on an individual" and "may not be relied upon as such against such a person" but found that Member States had responsibilities towards individuals not simply as public authorities but as employers. It found that the Area Health Authority was an "organ of the state" and that this phrase would cover all organs of the administration including Miss Marshall's employer, as part of the National Health Service. In this case, Miss Marshall was able to rely on the directive as having vertical direct effect.

In a series of subsequent cases, the Court continued to interpret the meaning of "organ of the state" as widely as possible to minimise the inequalities arising when individuals attempted to assert their Community rights against their employers and to prevent a Member State from relying as a defence on its own failure. Difficulties revolved round the question of whether the employer was a public authority (in which case an employee would be allowed to pursue a case based on the vertical direct effect of a directive) rather than a private business (where the employee would not be able to pursue their Community rights at all). See also:

- *Foster v British Gas plc* [1990]. This concerned a case brought in pursuance of rights guaranteed by the Equal Treatment Directive 76/207. The Court held that British Gas—a nationalised industry at that time rather than a private company—was an organ of the state as it was offering a public service under the control of a public authority, and was therefore open to challenge through vertical direct effect.
- *Johnston v Chief Constable of the Royal Ulster Constabulary* [1986]. It was held that a directive could be relied upon against a Chief Constable as he was responsible to the public for the maintenance of order and safety and was not acting as a private individual.

It was by now quite clear that an individual could pursue rights conferred by an unimplemented directive against a Member State through the doctrine of vertical direct effect. But inequalities of treatment depending on the status of the employer/alleged infringer remained. This was aggravated by Member States sometimes incorporating directives into national law using precisely the same wording as the original, thus giving them the appearance of regulations.

In *Faccini Dori v Recreb Srl* [1994], when the Court was asked once again to rule on horizontal direct effect, it resolved the uncertainty once and for all. It emphasised that extending the doctrine of direct effect of directives to individuals would be "to recognise a power in the Community to enact obligations with immediate effect"; a power which previously only related to regulations. To attribute horizontal direct effect to directives would therefore establish that they had the same legal effect as regulations. However, a Directive may produce effects analogous to horizontal direct effect in a very narrow and specific range of circumstances. This "incidental" horizontal direct effect, as it is called, may apply where there is a triangular relationship between the applicant, the state and other specified individuals who will be affected by the court decision (*CIA Security* [1996]: *Unilever* [2000]). However, the successful case law in this area appears to be limited to cases under Directive 83/189 and its replacement, Directive 98/34. Both these Directives require that Member States notify the Commission of national law technical standards and regulations that apply to goods. Where national law has not been notified in breach of the directive, that national law cannot be relied upon. This case law is highly controversial in that the practical effect is that the legal position of individuals is directly affected by the provisions of the directive. The case law, therefore, must be treated with caution and should be viewed as a very narrow exception to the general rule that Directives can never produce horizontal direct effect.

Although directives do not have horizontal direct effect, this does not mean that individuals are without legal redress. Rather, individuals may enforce their rights under a directive through the concept of indirect effect or through the *Francovich* principles of state liability (*see* under Member State Liability).

Indirect Effect

Despite the Court's insistence that provisions of Community law must have *effet utile,* the main limitations on the direct effect of directives are that legally binding European legislation:

- Must fulfil the *Van Gend en Loos* criteria—be sufficiently precise, unconditional and not involve discretion in the method of implementation;
- Cannot have direct effect until the time limit for implementation has expired;
- Cannot have direct effect unless a Member State has failed to implement or has incorrectly implemented the provisions of the directive into national law; and
- Does not have horizontal direct effect.

The Court therefore created an obligation on national courts to interpret national law in such a way as to achieve the aim of the directive. This approach—known as indirect effect—was based on Article 5 (now Article

10) which requires Member States to "take all appropriate measures, whether general or particular, to ensure fulfilment of the obligations arising out of this Treaty or resulting from action taken by the institutions of the Community."
In the case of *Von Colson und Kamman v Land Nordrhein-Westfalen* [1984] challenge was made under the Equal Treatment Directive 76/207. The Court of Justice found that the directive was not sufficiently precise and unconditional to possess direct effect but invoked Article 5 which placed Member States under an obligation to fulfil their Treaty obligations, stating that national implementing legislation had to be sufficient "such as to guarantee real and effective judicial protection" and that "it was for the national court to interpret and apply the legislation adopted ... in conformity with the requirements of Community law, insofar as it is given discretion to do so under national law".

This approach was extended in *Marleasing SA v La Commercial Internacional de Alimentacion SA* [1990] a case brought by one company against another. As well as reiterating the prohibition against horizontal direct effect, the Court repeated the obligation on national courts to interpret national legislation whether adopted before or after the directive as far as possible in the light of the wording and purpose of the directive.

The interpretative obligation has proved problematic for national courts in the situation where they are obliged to interpret national legislation that predates a directive (*Litster v Forth Dry Dock Engineering* [1990]). Nevertheless, the Court of Justice has consistently held that the interpretative obligation applies regardless of whether the disputed national law was enacted before or after the European law and whether it was enacted for the purpose of complying with EU law or not. Clearly, there are limits to the appropriateness and usefulness of this interpretative obligation, especially in the situation where national law expressly contradicts the Directive (*Wagner Miret* [1993]).

The Court of Justice has also made it clear that indirect effect cannot be used in criminal proceedings (*Kolpinghuis Nijmegen* [1987]; *Arcaro* [1996]).

Additionally, the Court has confirmed that during the period in which Member States have discretion to implement national law to give effect to the directive, they must refrain from taking action which undermines the aims and objectives of the directive and/or the Treaty (*Mangold* [2006]).

Direct Effect of Recommendations and Opinions
Since Recommendations and Opinions do not produce binding legal effects, they cannot produce direct effects (*Grimaldi* [1989]).

MEMBER STATE LIABILITY

After a series of cases in which horizontal direct effect was denied, the Court then turned in a different direction to protect individuals' Community rights. Individuals who had suffered as a result of a Member State's failure to fulfil its Community obligations had at that stage little redress in law, other than to rely on a national court making a preliminary reference to the European Court of Justice on the interpretation of the Treaty.

In 1991 with the landmark case of *Francovich*, it began to build a system of Member State liability as a default position to provide effective rights for individuals. The principle of Member State liability places an obligation upon a defaulting Member State to recompense individuals in damages for its own failure. Although in *Francovich*, Directive 80/987 (on the protection of workers in the event of the insolvency of their employer) was held not to be directly effective, the Court held that the protection of Community rights would be weakened if individuals were unable to obtain any effective remedy when their rights were infringed by a breach of Community law for which a Member State could be held responsible. It laid down three conditions to be fulfilled before a Member State might be found to be liable in damages even if the measure was not directly effective:

- The directive must confer rights for the benefits of individuals;
- The content of the rights must be identifiable from the directive; and
- There must be a causal link between the damage suffered and the breach.

The Court did not decide how the extent of liability was to be determined. This was to be a matter for the national courts to determine—though national procedures had "to ensure the full protection of rights which individuals might derive from Community law".

The implications of the *Francovich* judgment were that Member States faced the possibility of paying compensation to individuals if they failed to implement a directive in time. But some areas of doubt remained; whether any other type of breach of Community law by Member States other than a failure to implement a directive would lead to Member States incurring liability in damages; and secondly, whether "fault" was necessary in order to incur liability.

Where the Court has found a Member State to have a wide discretion, that is to say the competent national authorities have substantive choices in how they can act under Community law, it has applied the *Factortame (No. 3)* conditions. These were set out in joined cases *Brasserie du Pêcheur v Germany* and *R v Secretary of State for Transport, Ex p. Factortame* [1996] in which the Court considered claims for compensation as a result of conflicting national and Community law. These conditions were that:

- The rule of law infringed must be intended to confer rights on individuals;
- The breach must be sufficiently serious; and
- There must be a direct causal link between the breach of the obligation resting on the state and the damage sustained by the injured parties.

The requirements for establishing state liability are clearly similar to those arising from *Francovich* with the added requirement of establishing a "sufficiently serious" breach. The Court clarified what it meant by this and provided guidelines for national courts to evaluate whether or not a breach was sufficiently serious as follows:

- How clear and precise was the rule which was breached?
- Did national authorities have any discretion in its implementation?
- Was the breach intentional?
- Was the error of law excusable?
- Had a Community institution contributed to the breach?

The decisive test on whether or not a breach was sufficiently serious would be whether or not the Member State had manifestly and gravely disregarded the limits of its discretion.

In *R v Ministry of Agriculture, Fisheries and Food, Ex p. Hedley Lomas (Ireland) Ltd* [1994], the Court applied the *Factortame (No. 3)* conditions. The Ministry of Agriculture, Fisheries and Food had refused licences for the exporting of livestock to Spain because it believed that Spain was acting contrary to Directive 74/557. The UK was held to have breached Community law by imposing an export ban contrary to Article 34 (now Article 29). It had clearly acted in the face of Community law and accordingly was liable in damages to Hedley Lomas.

In *R v HM Treasury, Ex p. British Telecommunications plc* [1996], the issue was the incorrect implementation of a directive by the UK where it clearly did not have wide discretion in its Community obligation to implement a directive correctly. In this case though, the directive at issue was imprecisely worded and the UK had acted in good faith. The breach was held not to be sufficiently serious enough to incur liability for damages.

However, in *Dillenkofer v Federal Republic of Germany* [1996] Germany had failed to implement Directive 90/314 in time. The type of breach was therefore similar to that in *Francovich*. The Court went on to apply the *Factortame (No. 3)* conditions rather than the original *Francovich* conditions, thus indicating that it regarded the conditions relating to state liability to be fixed no matter what the nature of the breach was. In this case, it stated that the very nature of Germany's breach of Community law—a complete disregard of its obligations—was sufficiently serious.

To provide an effective mechanism for the enforcement of individuals' rights, ensure consistent application of Community law throughout the Member States and to encourage Member States to be vigilant in their application of Community law, the Court of Justice has now established that the requirements for state liability are that:

(1) Based on a Member State's obligations under Article 10 it must "take all appropriate measures ... to ensure fulfilment of the obligations arising out of this Treaty ... (and) facilitate the achievement of the Community's tasks. (It) shall abstain from any measure which could jeopardise the attainment of the objectives of this Treaty."

(2) A breach of Community law is *sufficiently serious* where, in the exercise of its legislative powers, a Member State has manifestly and gravely disregarded the limits on the exercise of its powers. If, at the time when it committed the infringement, the Member State in question did not have legislative choices and had only considerably reduced, or even no discretion, the mere infringement of Community law may be sufficient to establish the existence of a sufficiently serious breach.

(3) The nature of a sufficiently serious breach of a Member State's obligations does not necessarily require to be non-implementation of a directive. Such a breach could include instances of actions by a Member State:

- After a judgment by the Court finding it in breach of Community law;
- Where it had persisted in its actions despite that judgment;
- Where it had taken no action to implement a directive; and
- Where it had acted (or omitted to act) in the face of established Community law.

(4) Fault—whether negligent or intentional—is not in one of the conditions which it is necessary to satisfy in order for state liability to be established, especially since the concept of "fault" may differ throughout the various legal systems of the Member States.

(5) It is for the national courts to determine whether a breach of Community law is sufficiently serious to incur the non-contractual liability of a Member State vis-à-vis individuals.

SUPREMACY

Creating an effective legal system to apply directly within the Member States in a uniform and consistent manner would be of little value if Member States themselves could enact conflicting measures which would override Community law or choose which Community rules they would—or would not—apply. Nor were the founding Treaties of any assistance, as they contained no express provision on how to deal with the possibility of a conflict between a rule of Community law and national provisions. The basis of the Court's deduction of the supremacy of Community law therefore was to rely on Article 5 (now Article 10) of the Treaty, which set out the obligations of the Member States to ensure its effectiveness and by implication, the effectiveness of legislation enacted in furtherance of Treaty objectives.

In the case of *Costa v ENEL* [1964], Mr Costa challenged a small electricity bill from the Italian State electricity authority, arguing that the Italian legislation nationalising the electricity industry infringed both the Italian Constitution and the provisions of the EEC Treaty. In a much quoted statement, the Court held that:

"By creating a Community of unlimited duration, having its own institutions, its own personality, its own legal capacity and capacity of representation on the international plane and more particularly, real powers stemming from a limitation of sovereignty or a transfer of powers from the States of the Community, the Member States have limited their sovereign rights, albeit within limited fields, and have thus created a body of law which binds both their nationals and themselves.

The integration into the laws of each Member States of provisions which derive from the Community, and more generally the terms and the spirit of the Treaty *make it impossible for the States,* as a corollary, *to accord precedence to a unilateral and subsequent measure over a legal system accepted by them.*" [emphasis added]

The supremacy of Community law was given further weight in *Internationale Handelsgesellschaft* [1970] and in *Simmenthal* [1977] in which the Court went further and stated that:

"Any National Court must … apply Community law in its entirety… and must accordingly set aside any provision of national law which may conflict with it, whether prior or subsequent to the Community rule."

In the UK, the European Communities Act 1972 provides for the supremacy of Community law by accepting the legal effect of Community provisions in the UK. The same applies to judgments of the Court of Justice concerning interpretation on the meaning and effect, or validity of any Community measure. In relation to Acts of the UK Parliament, this means that directly applicable Community measures prevail even over future Acts of Parliament, if the latter are inconsistent with Community law. It also means that by ratifying the European Treaties, the UK, like any other Member State must refrain from enacting legislation inconsistent with Community law. In 1991, in *Factortame (No. 2)* the Court of Justice replied to a question put by the UK House of Lords:

"Community law must be interpreted as meaning that a national court which, in a case before it concerning Community law, considers that the sole obstacle which precludes it from granting interim relief is a rule of national law, must set aside that rule."

Nevertheless, accepting supremacy of Community law—whether a Treaty Article, secondary legislation or agreement with a third state—has raised difficulties in some Member States over the years, particularly with respect to previously enacted national law or the provisions of a Member State's own constitution.

The role of the Court of Justice was pivotal in settling the issues which arose. Interpreting Community law was entrusted by the Treaty solely to the Court and through its case law the concept of primacy of Community law now means that:

- States have agreed through their membership of the European Community to the limitation of their sovereign rights, *Costa v ENEL* [1964];
- Community law may not be invalidated by any provisions of national constitutions, *Internationale Handelsgesellschaft* [1970];
- Previously enacted but conflicting national law must be repealed, *Commission v France (re French Merchant Seamen)* [1974];
- Community law must be applied immediately without waiting for inconsistent national law to be repealed, *Simmenthal* [1977];
- Member States may not plead *force majeure*, *Commission v Italy (Second Art Treasures case)* [1971];
- Supremacy applies regardless of whether the inconsistent national law is civil or criminal in nature, *Procureur du Roi v Dassonville* [1974];
- National courts should interpret national legislation so as to comply with the Member State's Community obligations whether the national law is passed before or after the relevant provision of Community law, *Marleasing* [1990]; and
- This obligation must not be applied retrospectively to penalise individuals, *Kolpinghuis Nijmegen* [1987].

SUBSIDIARITY

In an attempt to demonstrate that the relationship between Community law and national law was not one which irrevocably transferred the centre of power from national governments to Community institutions, in 1993 the Treaty on European Union formally introduced the principle of subsidiarity into the EC Treaty by inserting Article 3(b) (now Article 5) into the principles of the Community. It set out that:

> "in areas which do not fall within its exclusive competence, the Community shall take action, in accordance with the principle of subsidiarity, only if and insofar as the objectives of the proposed action cannot be sufficiently achieved by Member States and can therefore by reason of the scale or effects of the proposed action, be better achieved by the Community."

In essence, this meant that the choice of legislative or other action was required to be taken in favour of Member States in cases where:

- Legislative or other action required to be taken by either the Member States or the Community;
- The Treaty did not specify that the Community possessed the power to act;
- The powers could be exercised by a Member State more effectively and in proportion to the objective pursued; and
- The need for action at Community level could not be demonstrated.

In the face of some confusion over aspects of the application of this principle, a Protocol on the Application of the Principles of Subsidiarity and Proportionality attached to the Treaty of Amsterdam set out that:

> "*for Community action to be justified* both aspects of the subsidiarity principle shall be met: the objectives of the proposed action cannot be sufficiently achieved by Member States' action in the framework of their national constitutional system and can therefore be better achieved by action on the part of the Community. The following guidelines should be used in examining whether the above-mentioned condition is fulfilled:
>
> - The issue under consideration has transnational aspects which cannot be satisfactorily regulated by action by Member States;
> - Actions by Member States alone or lack of Community action would conflict with the requirements of the Treaty (such as the need to correct distortion of competition or avoid disguised restrictions on trade or strengthen economic and social cohesion) or would otherwise significantly damage Member States' interests;
> - Action at Community level would produce clear benefits by reason of its scale or effects compared with action at the level of the Member States.

The form of Community action shall be as simple as possible, consistent with satisfactory achievement of the objective of the measure and the need for effective enforcement. The Community shall legislate only to the extent necessary. Other things being equal, Directives should be preferred to regulations and Framework Directives to detailed measures...

Regarding the nature and the extent of Community action, Community measures should leave as much scope for national decision as possible, consistent with securing the aim of the measure and observing the requirements of the Treaty ...

Where the application of the principle of subsidiarity leads to no action being taken by the Community, Member States are required in their action to comply with the general rules laid down in Article 5 (now Article 10) of the Treaty by taking all appropriate measures to ensure fulfilment of their obligations under the Treaty and by abstaining from any measure which could jeopardise the attainment of the objectives of the Treaty." [emphasis added]

As the institutions primarily concerned in the legislative process, the Commission, the Council and Parliament have express responsibility for demonstrating the effective application of this principle. For any provision which falls under the principle and after "consulting widely", the Commission must justify the relevance of its proposals with regard to subsidiarity and detail this in its explanatory memorandum. Compliance with Article 10 of the Commission proposals must be specifically addressed by the Council and the European Parliament during the passage of legislation. In the preamble to the measure in question, reasons demonstrating its compliance with the principles of subsidiarity and proportionality must be set out.

Despite the Protocol, application of this Treaty provision has not been without its problems. Issues relating to its political relevance in the division of powers between the Community and its Member States and whether an action for judicial review can be founded on the issue of subsidiarity have still not been satisfactorily resolved.

---

7. JUDICIAL REVIEW

To protect the rights of individuals and Member States, the Treaty provides for an extensive system of judicial review to ensure that Community institutions fulfil their obligations under the Treaty in a proper manner. Based on French administrative law, judicial review also safeguards the rights of the institutions in their dealings with one another. The Treaty confers specific powers and duties on each of the institutions which they must exercise according to the Treaty:

- Under Article 230, the Court of Justice may consider an action for annulment of an act of the institutions;
- Article 232 provides the means by which an institution's failure to act may be investigated; and
- Article 241 provides a means of indirect review where the "plea of illegality" is invoked

By far the most important of these three is the action for annulment under Article 230.

ACTION FOR ANNULMENT UNDER ARTICLE 230

Article 230

"The Court of Justice shall review the legality of acts adopted jointly by the European Parliament and the Council, of acts of the Council, of the Commission and of the ECB, other than recommendations and opinions, and of acts of the European Parliament intended to produce legal effects vis-à-vis third parties.

It shall for this purpose have jurisdiction in actions brought by a Member State, the European Parliament, the Council or the Commission on grounds of lack of competence, infringement of an essential procedural requirement, infringement of this Treaty or of any rule of law relating to its application, or misuse of powers.

The Court of Justice shall have jurisdiction under the same conditions in actions brought by the Court of Auditors and by the ECB for the purpose of protecting their prerogatives.

Any natural or legal person may, under the same conditions, institute proceedings against a decision addressed to that person or against a decision which, although in the form of a regulation or a decision addressed to another person, is of direct and individual concern to the former.

The proceedings provided for in this Article shall be instituted within two months of the publication of the measure, or of its notification to the plaintiff, or, in the absence thereof, of the day on which it came to the knowledge of the latter, as the case may be."

In order to be successful, the action for annulment brought under Article 230 must clear two hurdles. The first is the admissibility requirement. This means that the applicant must first satisfy the Court that he or she (or it, in the case of a business) is allowed to bring the action in the first place and that it is laid down within the time limits. This is known as *locus standi*. Secondly, the applicant must then convince the Court that the challenge is on one of the grounds for review which is allowed under Article 230.

The Treaty of Nice conferred jurisdiction on the Court of First Instance to hear most classes of direct actions such as in Article 230 (Annulment), Article 232 (Failure to Act), Article 235 (Non-contractual Liability of the Community), Article 236 (Staff Cases) and Article 238 (Arbitration Clauses). Actions brought by the Member States, the institutions and the European Central Bank are reserved for the Court of Justice.

To found a successful action, five questions must be addressed.

(1) Which Acts may be Challenged?

Anything which is legally binding—regulations, decisions, directives, but not Recommendations and Opinions (*see* Article 249). However, these forms of legislation are not all that may be challenged. Because the Court of Justice is concerned with the substance of a measure rather than the form it takes, it will consider all measures taken by the institutions which are designed to have legal effect. In *Commission v Council (re ERTA)* [1971], "discussions" of guidelines before the signing of the European Road Traffic Agreement were held to be capable of review by the Court. More recently, in *European Parliament v Council* [1994] the Court stated that:

> "annulment must be available in the case of all measures adopted by the institutions, whatever their nature or form, intended to have legal effects. It follows that an action ... is admissible irrespective of whether the act was adopted by the institution pursuant to the Treaty provisions."

However in *IBM v Commission* [1981], the company challenged a letter and Statement of Objections sent by the Commission in pursuance of competition rules. As this was only the first step of several in an enforcement procedure, the Court held that this could not be challenged. Only a final measure may be challenged.

(2) Who has the Right to Challenge?

A distinction is drawn between institutional and private applicants—between what are referred to as privileged applicants, limited privileged applicants and non-privileged applicants.

Privileged applicants are the Member States, the Council, the Commission and since the Treaty of Nice, the European Parliament. They have an automatic right to challenge any legal measure as they are presumed to have an interest in any Community proceedings (*Luxembourg v European Parliament* [1983]).

Limited privileged applicants are the European Central Bank and the Court of Auditors. They have a limited right to challenge measures, but only if they can demonstrate a specific interest in the proceedings and to safeguard their prerogatives (*European Parliament v Council* [1991]).

Private individuals and companies (natural or legal persons)—that is, non-privileged applicants—may challenge a Community act but only if this act is:

- A decision addressed to that person. This means that there is an obvious and straightforward right of challenge. If the addressee of the contested decision brings an action within the time limit, the claim will be admissible.
- A decision addressed to another person or to a Member State. In this case, the applicant must show that the act in question is of direct and individual concern to them (*Fiskano v Commission* [1994]).
- A decision in the form of a regulation. As can be deduced from Article 249, a regulation has "general application", that is, it applies not to a limited number of people, but a wide range, defined abstractly and unnamed. A "true" regulation may not be challenged (*Calpack* [1980]). Only decisions have the characteristic of binding those to whom they are addressed. Even if the measure is in the form of a regulation, it must be equivalent to a decision and apply to identifiable individuals and once more, it must be of direct and individual concern to the applicant (*International Fruit Co v Commission* [1970]).

Having established that the individual is in fact challenging a decision (or a decision in the form of a regulation), the next step is to establish direct and individual concern.

A measure is of direct concern to an applicant when a Member State is given no discretion to act under the disputed provision or when there is no implementing measure required to be acted upon by the Member State and the measure directly affects the legal situation of the individual (*Glencore Grain* [1998]). In *Bock* [1971] despite the fact that the German authorities had already informed the applicant that they would reject his application for an import licence for Chinese mushrooms as soon as the Commission allowed them to do so, it was held that Germany's discretion whether or not to authorise the import licence was not at issue as the Commission had upheld a refusal in response to Bock's application. Bock was held to be directly concerned.

It is of individual concern if it affects the applicant in the same way as if it had been addressed to him personally, either alone or as a member of a closed class. The test is that in *Plaumann* [1963]. Plaumann was a fruit importer. A decision sent by the Commission to Germany refused permission to reduce the duty on clementines imported from outside the Community. Plaumann challenged the Commission's decision. That his business would be affected was not sufficient to constitute "individual concern" within the meaning of Article 230. The Court said the measure was a response to a general problem and drafted accordingly, without special reference to any individual trader, present or potential. Plaumann was merely an importer and as anyone could set up in business as an importer, Plaumann was not therefore individually concerned, since the potential pool of individuals affected by the measure was open.

Although most applicants seeking to prove individual concern are unsuccessful, in the case of *Töpfer*, an importer of grain and cereals had requested a licence on October 1, 1963 from the German Government so that he could import cereals from France. He was refused permission and the Commission was asked to confirm this decision which it did, retrospectively, on October 4. The Court said that the identity of the applicant had been known to the Commission before October 4, and it was therefore in a position to know that its decision affected the interests of existing importers. This fact distinguished Töpfer since he was a member of a closed group of affected individuals. Töpfer was therefore individually concerned and accordingly his action was admissible.

In Bock's case in 1971, the Court held that the company was individually concerned because the application made to import Chinese mushrooms was made on September 11, refused by Germany on the same date but upheld by the Commission on September 15. The number and identity of importers concerned was already fixed and ascertainable before the refusal by the Commission on September 15, and it was in a position to know that its decision would affect the interests and situation of those importers alone.

The 1985 case of *Piraiki-Patriki* concerned seven Greek cotton companies which challenged a Commission decision allowing the French Government to impose a quota system on imports of yarn from Greece between November 1981 and January 1982. Some of the applicants had already signed contracts with French companies for deliveries above the quota during that period. The Court held that the decision was of individual concern to those of the applicants who had signed the contracts as they were "members of a limited class of traders identified or identifiable by the Commission and by reason of these contracts, particularly affected by the decision."

However, in the case of *Codorniu* in 1994, the Court of Justice developed its approach to "individual concern" further. The measure in question was in the form of a regulation made by the Council which reserved the term "crémant" for particular types of sparkling wine produced in France and Luxembourg. The applicant was a major producer of sparkling wines in Spain, one of the largest producers of sparkling wine in Europe and had held a Spanish trademark since 1924 for its Gran Crémant wine. The Court held that the measure was a true regulation of general application and although Codorniu was not one of a fixed and ascertainable group, he was distinguished from other producers as he would be deprived of the trademark right which he had held for the previous 70 years.

The Court reverted to its more restrictive approach as set out in *Plaumann* in the case of *Stichting Greenpeace Council* in 1998 which seemed to indicate that it was still difficult to get past the *locus standi* hurdle. Greenpeace had challenged a Commission decision to allocate financial aid to Spain to build two power stations in the Canary Islands on environmental grounds. The Court held that "the interests [of the local residents, fishermen and farmers] are by their very nature, common and shared, and the rights relating to these are liable to be held by a potentially large number of individuals so there could never be a closed class of applicants".

These restrictive rules on *locus standi* for private applicants have been unchanged since 1958, despite the Courts own misgivings about their continuance, set out in its submission to the 1996 IGC. In practice it is almost impossible for an individual to satisfy the admissibility test for a challenge under Article 230. Hope that the tide was at last turning came in the guise of *Jégo-Quéré et Cie* [2002]. In that case, the Court of First Instance deviated from the prior case law, relaxing the previously restrictive application of "individual concern". However, later that year, the Court of Justice in *Unión de Pequeños Agricultores* [2002] reiterated that the pre-*Jégo-Quéré* case law was still to apply. It emphasised that it was not for the Court to reform the conditions for *locus standi* and that if Member States wished to liberalise the rules regulating the right of individuals to challenge Community measures, then it would have to be secured by way of Treaty amendment. Thus, at present, the restrictive rules on standing remain.

(3) What are the Grounds for Challenge?

Lack of Competence

The Treaty requires each of the Community institutions to act within the limits of the powers conferred upon it. Thus in the *ERTA* case [1989], it was obvious to the Court that the Council lacked the power to negotiate the European Road Transport Agreement, as Article 300 states that the Commission negotiates international agreements and the Council concludes them. It follows that every act of a Community institution must clearly indicate on which Treaty provision it is based (*Germany v EP and Council (Tobacco Advertising)* [2000]).

Infringement of an Essential Procedural Requirement
Institutions adopting binding measures must adhere to the correct procedures
as laid down either in the Treaty or within secondary legislation implemented
in accordance with the Treaty. The leading case, *Roquette Frères* [1980]
concerned a requirement for Parliament to be consulted in a legal measure.
"Failure to consult" annulled the measure in question.

"Failure to give sufficient reasons" may also be grounds for annulment of
a binding measure. This ground of review is normally pleaded when an
institution has not given reasons for its adoption of binding legal measures
(*Commission v Council Re Titanium Dioxide Waste* [1991]). The measure
must therefore specify the principal issues of fact and law in a clear and
concise manner so that the reasoning which led the institution to make its
choice of legal basis may be clearly understood.

Infringement of the Treaty or of any Rule relating to its Application
This ground of challenge is interpreted broadly because it covers not only the
Treaties and their implementing legislation, but also general principles of law
such as:

- Equality (*R Louwage v Commission* [1974]);
- Legal certainty (*Openbaar Ministerie v Bout* [1982]);
- Proportionality (*Commission v Germany* [1994]);
- Fundamental rights (now expressly set out in Article 6(1) of the Treaty
  on European Union); and
- Legitimate expectation (*Töpfer* [1965]).

Misuse of Powers
This refers to an act of an institution endeavouring to achieve an objective
which is not that for which the original powers were conferred upon it
(*Giuffrida v Commission* [1976]). The Court will examine:

- The purpose the act was intended to achieve; and
- The purpose of the provision under which the act was adopted, to see if
  the act followed this purpose.

This ground is the most difficult to prove as evidence is required that the
intention of the institution in question was different from that stated in the
contested measure (*Crispoltoni* [1994]).

(4) What are the Relevant Time Limits?
The Court enforces the time limits very strictly. An applicant—whether
privileged or non-privileged—must bring a claim within two months of the
date of publication, or the date it was notified to the pursuer or the date he
became aware of it. This two month time limit is extended to take account of
the distance of the applicant from the Court in Luxembourg. A 10 day
extension is granted for the UK. A further 14 day extension comes into effect
when the measure is published in the Official Journal. However, in
exceptional circumstances, the applicant may be granted an extension, for
example in the case of *force majeure* (*Bayer* [1994]).

Regulations, directives and decisions adopted in accordance with the co-
decision procedure must be published in the Official Journal along with
Council and Commission Regulations and Directives of these institutions

which are addressed to all Member States. Other directives and decisions only require to be notified to those to whom they are addressed. They enter into force on the day specified in the act or if this is not specified, on the 20th day following publication.

If there is no challenge within the time limit, the measure is "good forever" and any challenge is inadmissible.

(5) What are the Consequences of Annulment?

Article 231 provides that if the action brought under Article 230 is successful, the Court shall declare the measure void from the very beginning. The Court has no power to order the institution concerned to take any particular steps but the institution is required under Article 233 to take the measures necessary to comply with the Court's judgment and therefore to endeavour to recreate the situation which would have existed had the measure not been adopted.

If the measure is a regulation, only the offending parts may be annulled (Article 231(2)); (*Société de Vente de Ciments et Bétons v Kerpen & Kerpen* [1983]) or the offending measure can remain in force until its replacement (*Timex v Council* [1985]), or, to preserve legal certainty the annulment only applies to the parties concerned in the case (*Simmenthal* [1979]).

APPEAL AGAINST FAILURE OF AN INSTITUTION TO ACT UNDER ARTICLE 232

Article 232

"Should the European Parliament, the Council or the Commission, in infringement of this Treaty, fail to act, the Member States and the other institutions of the Community may bring an action before the Court of Justice to have the infringement established.

This action shall be admissible only if the institution concerned has first been called upon to act. If, within two months of being so called upon, the institution concerned has not defined its position, the action may be brought within a further period of two months.

Any natural or legal person may, under the conditions laid down in the preceding paragraphs, complain to the Court of Justice that an institution of the Community has failed to address to that person any act other than a recommendation or an opinion.

The Court of Justice shall have jurisdiction, under the same conditions, in actions or proceedings brought by the ECB in the areas falling within the latter's field of competence and in actions or proceedings brought against the latter."

(1) What may be Challenged?

Actions under Article 232 can be regarded as "the other side of the coin" from actions under Article 230. While judicial review under Article 230 may annul acts of the institutions, failure to act under Article 232 may be used to compel an institution to fulfil its Community obligations. An action will thus *only be available where the applicant can show that such an obligation exists.*

The action for failure to act on the part of the European Parliament, the Council or the Commission can also be pleaded in the same action as that for annulment under Article 230. An apparent inconsistency between the two can be resolved by applying the "unity principle" whereby the Court has stated that "both provisions merely prescribe one and the same method of recourse" (*Chevalley v Commission* [1970]).

(2) Who has the Right to Challenge?

As with Article 230, there is a distinction between the status of applicants. In this case, Parliament is placed on the same footing as Member States and the right of action is given to "other institutions" of the Community. Individuals may only challenge a failure to act when it concerns a binding act of which they would have been the addressee (*Mackprang v Commission* [1971]) and in which they are able to establish direct and individual concern (*ENU v Commission* [1993]).

(3) What are the Relevant Time Limits?

Although the Treaty does not specify any time limit during which an action must be initiated, the applicant must approach the institution concerned beforehand and make it quite clear that if, within a two month time limit, it does not comply with its Community obligations to act, it will be subject to a challenge under Article 232. Once this approach has been made the institution concerned has a period of two months within which to define its position. Most cases will be closed at this stage. If the institution does not define its position, the applicant has a further two months within which to bring the action.

(4) What are the Consequences of a Successful Challenge?

If the application under Article 232 is upheld, the Court will declare that the failure to act is contrary to the Treaty and Article 233 requires that the institution must "take the necessary measures to comply with the judgment of the Court of Justice" within a reasonable period of time. If, however, the institution has defined its position but not adopted the disputed measure, it is not possible to bring an action for "failure to act" (*Lütticke* [1966]).

PLEA OF ILLEGALITY UNDER ARTICLE 241

Article 241

"Notwithstanding the expiry of the period laid down in ... Article 230, any party, may, in proceedings in which a regulation adopted jointly by the European Parliament and the Council, or a regulation of the Council, of the Commission, or of the ECB is at issue, plead the grounds specified in ... Article 230 in order to invoke before the Court of Justice the inapplicability of that regulation."

This Treaty Article also provides for a challenge to the act of an institution, in this case, a regulation. Unlike Articles 230 and 232, a plea of illegality under Article 241 is an indirect action. It is only available as a defence where other proceedings have been brought against the applicant and may be pleaded only in the course of proceedings which are already underway on other grounds. Because of the restrictive nature of *locus standi* for the action of annulment under Article 230, the individual may not mount a direct challenge to a regulation. However, in the course of Article 230 proceedings challenging a decision, provided he overcomes the admissibility hurdle, he may claim that the original regulation on which the decision is based, is illegal. This action has also been held to covers acts of the institutions which produce similar effects to those of regulations but which do not actually take the form of regulations (*Simmenthal* [1979]).

If the Article 241 plea succeeds, although the regulation itself will not be annulled, its basis for the decision in question will be "inapplicable" and the decision will be void.

---

8. PRELIMINARY RULINGS

Giving effect to Community law as set out by the Treaties and ensuring its provisions would be applied throughout the Member States by all national courts in a uniform and consistent manner was essential to the authors of the Community Treaties if the proper functioning of the common market was to be achieved and preserved. To that end, Article 234 enables national courts and tribunals to refer questions of Community law that require to be decided in a case pending before them to the Court of Justice for a ruling. This procedure has also proved to be the springboard for the development of some of the most fundamental concepts of Community law, such as direct effect and supremacy.

Notwithstanding the advances made for the benefit of individuals seeking to enforce their Community rights within their own national courts through the doctrine of direct effect, the preliminary ruling procedure has allowed them to mount challenges to the validity of Community acts in a manner which is much less restrictive than the procedural requirements of judicial review.

This preliminary rulings procedure is not one which an individual may use to bring his case direct. It is an "indirect action". It involves the national court hearing a case concerning a point of Community law and asking for guidance on its interpretation from the Court of Justice. In the future, the Court of First Instance may be granted jurisdiction over certain 234 actions by virtue of Article 225(3) of the EC Treaty. The system of preliminary rulings represents a dialogue between a national court and the Court of Justice. The parties in the case cannot ask a national judge to make a request for a preliminary ruling to Luxembourg.

The procedure involves a national court seeking guidance on a point of interpretation, or validity of European law by formulating a question (or questions) for clarification by the Court of Justice. The case in the national court is then suspended until a ruling is given. The Court of Justice does not investigate the facts of the case, nor does it apply the law to the case. It simply clarifies the point of European law. The judgment is binding on the national court referring the question which then continues the case and in due course, gives judgment in the light of the European Court's interpretation of the law.

Article 234 itself provides a great deal of information on who may use it and when questions should be referred. It reads as follows:

> "The Court of Justice shall have jurisdiction to give preliminary rulings concerning the interpretation of this Treaty; the validity and interpretation of acts of the institutions of the Community and of the ECB; the interpretation of the statutes of bodies established by an act of the Council, where those statutes so provide.
>
> Where such a question is raised before any court or tribunal of a Member State, that court or tribunal may, if it considers that a decision on the question is necessary to enable it to give judgment, request the Court of Justice to give a ruling thereon.
>
> Where any such question is raised in a case pending before a court or tribunal of a Member State against whose decisions there is no judicial remedy under national law, that court or tribunal shall bring the matter before the Court of Justice."

The power of the Court therefore falls into two main groups, first is the Court's interpretation of Community law and second is its power to rule on the validity of the acts of the institutions. Note that in common with other constitutional courts, the Court of Justice does not have the power to call into question the validity of the founding constitutional texts, in this case the EC Treaty and the Treaty of the European Union.

THE INTERPRETATION OF COMMUNITY LAW

Under Article 234(1), the Court of Justice has jurisdiction to interpret:

- The Treaties (the European Community Treaty and the Euratom Treaty);
- All the Acts of the institutions, whether legally binding or not; and
- International agreements which are concluded by the Community with third countries.

The main interpretative techniques of the Court of Justice are contextual and teleological. Though it always starts with the text of the Treaty and places the object and purpose of the provision in question within its context in relation to other provisions, the Court may also look at the general scheme of the Treaty as a whole and at its broad policy objectives, even though these are set out in very general terms in the main.

THE VALIDITY OF THE ACTS OF THE INSTITUTIONS

According to the judgment in *Grad* [1970], national courts are empowered to submit to the European Court all questions regarding validity of all measures without distinction. The Court can therefore rule on the validity of regulations, directives, decisions, recommendations and opinions.

Although the wording of Article 234(1) mentions "validity", Article 230 governing the system of judicial review concerns "legality" and so with these two Articles the Court has created a complete system of legal remedies to review all the acts of the institutions (*Les Verts v European Parliament* [1986]).

Unlike the four grounds of review under Article 230, Article 234 does not contain any restrictions as to grounds on which validity of Community acts may be contested (*International Fruit Co. (No. 3)* [1972]).

As opposed to the time limitation by which cases for judicial review may be lodged, questions of validity may be raised under Article 234 at any time.

The finding of the Court through a preliminary ruling is binding on the parties to the case in the national courts, but if an act of an institution is declared invalid, it is normally retroactive as under Article 230 from when the act was originally adopted. If it is declared invalid, it is invalid throughout the Community.

There is nothing in the wording of Article 234 to say who may declare a Community act invalid. In the case of *Foto-Frost* [1987], the Court stated that national courts may consider the validity of a Community act. If it is clearly valid, they may make a statement to this effect, though a national court cannot declare a Community act to be invalid. As a requirement of legal certainty, this is a prerogative of the Court of Justice which it will exercise through the preliminary ruling procedure.

Article 234(2) contains the provision for an optional or discretionary reference to the Court of Justice. When a matter comes before a national court it may refer a question though it is not obliged to do so.

"Where such a question is raised before any court or tribunal of a member state, that court or tribunal may, if it considers that a decision on the question is necessary to enable it to give judgment, request the Court of Justice to give a ruling thereon."

The national court must therefore establish the facts of the case before it. If an issue of Community law is critical to its final determination of the case and it does not have complete confidence in its ability to resolve the issue itself, it should refer the question to the Court of Justice. It should bear in mind the differences between national and Community legislation, the need for uniform interpretation throughout the Community and of the great advantages enjoyed by the Court of Justice in construing Community measures (*R v International Stock Exchange Ex p. Else* [1993]).

The Court of Justice does not enquire into the reasons why the national court has made a reference (*Costa v ENEL*), however the Court will not hear cases in which there is no real dispute between the parties nor will it answer purely hypothetical questions. (*Foglia v Novello* [1980]; *Schulte* [2005]). If it were to do this, it would jeopardise the whole purpose of Article 234. The Court may also reformulate the question posed.

As a matter of Community law, national courts have an absolute and unfettered discretion to refer which cannot be removed (*Auroux* [2007]). Thus any attempt to influence the Courts in this matter by Parliament or government would be unlawful.

In Article 234 (3), there is provision for a compulsory reference:

"Where any such question is raised before any court or tribunal of a Member State against whose decisions there is no judicial remedy under national law, that court or tribunal shall bring the matter before the Court of Justice."

The difference in the two paragraphs hinges on the words "may" and "shall". "May" means it is optional, at the discretion of the national court and "shall" conveys the imperative.

With a compulsory reference, the key words are "a court against whose decisions there is no judicial remedy". In these cases, if a question of Community law—interpretation or validity of a measure—is raised before a court from which there is no appeal, then that court is bound to send a question to the European Court. Failure of a national court to do so will invoke the liability of the Member State (*Traghetti* [2006]).The purpose of this goes to the heart of Article 234. It will avoid a mistaken interpretation of Community law being given by the highest courts in the land, other courts being bound by that decision through the doctrine of precedent. In other words, it prevents a body of national case law coming into existence in any Member State which is not in accordance with Community law. And, as with the whole of Article 234, it ensures the uniform interpretation and application of the law.

A compulsory referral from a court from which there is no appeal also ensures that if a lower court has not made a reference to the Court of Justice—which it is perfectly entitled to do under Article 234(2)—this is the final stage where any errors of law can be corrected.

So which actual courts in a Member State are subject to the obligation to refer? The problems which have arisen in this respect have led to the development of two theories:

(1) Only national courts which are always a court of last resort in the hierarchy of judicial precedent. For example, in Scotland the House of Lords for civil matters. This is the abstract theory.

(2) Any court which is a court of last resort in the case in question. This would include for example cases in the English Court of Appeal or the Scottish Court of Session when leave of appeal to the House of Lords has been refused. This is known as the concrete theory (*see R v Henn and Derby* [1979]).

Article 234(2) also mentions the words "any court or tribunal". When is a body a court or tribunal, and when is it not? Cases have come to the European Court from quasi-judicial bodies and the question was to establish their *locus standi*—whether or not they were allowed even to refer a case to the Court of Justice.

Courts of law within the judicial hierarchy of a Member State have automatic status. Whether other bodies such as arbitration tribunals and appeals committees, for example, had *locus standi* was more problematic. In the case of *Walter Schmid* [2002], the Court of Justice set out the essential characteristics of a "court or tribunal" within the Community context. The criteria to be used to measure whether this was so were that the body:

- Is established by law;
- Is permanent;
- Has compulsory jurisdiction;
- Its procedure is *inter pares;*

- Applies the rule of law; and
- Is independent.

The right to refer questions to the Court of Justice belongs to national "courts or tribunals" only. Parliaments, governments and Community institutions do not have locus standi to submit questions for preliminary rulings.

Article 234(3) lays down an obligatory referral in cases where there "is no judicial remedy". National supreme courts are understandably reluctant to constantly refer questions on issues where they believe the European Court has already clarified the point. The Court of Justice itself has recognised that there may be occasions where it is not necessary to make a preliminary ruling. This relaxation of the strict nature of Article 234(3), *acte clair*, is based on French administrative law. It means that no question of interpretation is necessary where a provision is quite clear. The Court described the circumstances in which a national court need not refer a question in the case of *CILFIT* [1982]:

- Where a question of Community law is irrelevant to the case at issue;
- The point has already been decided by a previous decision of the Court of Justice;
- If the correct application of Community law is so obvious as to leave no doubt as to the manner in which the matter is to be resolved; and
- The matter is equally obvious to the Courts of the other Member States and to the Court of Justice.

The Court went on to set out the problems were a national supreme court to decide not to ask for a preliminary ruling in these circumstances:

- Community law is drafted in several different languages all of them equally authentic and binding, so any interpretation by a national court would require a comparison of all different language versions;
- Community law has its own particular terminology, legal concepts do not necessarily have the same meaning in Community law as they do in national law; and
- Community law must always be interpreted in context and in the light of the purposes of the treaties as a whole, of the objectives of Community law and the evolution of Community law at that particular time, in other words, interpretation is by the teleological method.

Now that Community law is becoming more and more familiar to national judges, it is not unusual for the national supreme courts to use the doctrine of *acte clair* and decide cases containing a point of Community law without referring to the Court in Luxembourg (*British Fuels v Baxendale* [1999]).

To ensure that national courts are fully aware of the circumstances and the manner in which references should be made under Article 234, the Court of Justice is empowered to issue guidance notes. The most recent Information Note was issued in 2005 ([2005] O.J. C 143/1).

In addition, the Rules of Procedure of the Court of Justice have been amended in order to simplify the procedure for cases in which questions referred by a national court are identical to questions that have already been answered, where the answer to the question can be clearly deduced from existing case law or where the answer admits of no reasonable doubt. In these cases, the Court of Justice may give its decision by reasoned order. It may also:

- Request from the parties all such information relating to the facts and any other relevant documents; and
- Request clarification from national courts which refer questions to it for a preliminary ruling.

The Court has also set up an accelerated procedure where a matter is considered to be of exceptional urgency to restrict the matters requiring a ruling to essential points of law.

The effect of a preliminary ruling is to bind the national court in the case in which the reference was made and any other national court considering the same point of law.

The preliminary rulings procedure:

- Gives individuals the opportunity for an indirect challenge to the validity of Community law within their own national courts;
- Allows an individual to obtain domestic remedies which would otherwise not be available in the event of a direct challenge under Article 230;
- Is a Court-to-Court dialogue only;
- Provides guidance to a national court when applying the law;
- Is not an appeals procedure;
- Allows Community law to be interpreted by one authoritative source in a consistent and uniform manner throughout all Member States;
- Has allowed the Court of Justice to extend the scope and effectiveness of the Community legal order;
- Is not limited to the four grounds of review essential under Article 230;
- May be raised by a national court at any time;
- Must be raised by a national court or tribunal (within the Community context) unless the national court applies the *acte clair* doctrine; and
- Binds the court or tribunal which made the reference to the Court of Justice.

---

9. FREE MOVEMENT OF GOODS

Customs duties represent one of the oldest forms of national trade protection so it was hardly surprising that these and other such charges were one of the first obstacles that the Treaty set about removing to create a Europe-wide internal market based on unimpeded movement of goods across the whole Community. Ensuring the free movement of goods is an area of law illustrating how the Court and the Community legislators—the Commission, the Parliament and the Council—combine to attain a fundamental objective of the Community.

Article 3(1)(a) declares that:

"For the purposes set out in Article 2, the activities of the Community shall include ... the prohibition, as between Member States, of customs duties and quantitative restrictions on the import and export of goods and of all other measures having equivalent effect".

This aim of establishing an integrated market can easily be frustrated by Member States practising forms of protectionism designed to shield their national industries from the competitive pressures of imports. The most obvious way in which this is done is by making imports more expensive or setting invisible barriers such as different product, consumer and environmental standards. In order to prohibit these and other protectionist practices, the Treaty has identified three areas to guard against Member States erecting barriers to free movement of goods. The rules apply both to goods which originate in a Member State and to those which come from a third country and are in free circulation within a Member State.

Although the prohibitions restricting free movement of goods are addressed to Member States, the most important Articles of the Treaty within the area of free movement of goods are directly effective (*Van Gend en Loos* [1963]).

These three areas are prohibitions on:

- The imposition of customs duties (tariffs) and charges having equivalent effect to customs duties—Articles 3(a), 23 and 25;
- Discriminatory internal taxation—Article 90; and
- Quantitative restrictions on imports and exports (bans and quotas) and measures having an equivalent effect to quantitative restrictions—Articles 3(a), 28, 29, 30 and 95.

CUSTOMS DUTIES AND CHARGES HAVING EQUIVALENT EFFECT TO CUSTOMS DUTIES

Article 23

"(1) The Community shall be based upon a customs union which shall cover all trade in goods and which shall involve the prohibition between Member States of customs duties on imports and exports and of all charges having equivalent effect, and the adoption of a common customs tariff in their relations with third countries.

(2) The provisions of Article 25 and of Chapter 2 of this Title shall apply to products originating in Member States and to products coming from third countries which are in free circulation in Member States."

Externally, Article 23 refers to the Common Customs Tariff. Whenever goods cross an external border, the Common Customs Tariff is the same (set out in Commission Regulation 2658/87 which is regularly updated). Once it is paid, then the goods are in free circulation throughout the Member States. Member States do not have jurisdiction over the duty levied on goods from third countries. They may not amend the rate nor may they keep the proceeds which now belong to the Community as "own resources". Modification or suspension of the Common Customs Tariff is an exclusive Community matter and is decided by the Council.

From an internal, Community perspective, Article 23 means that Member States must abolish two types of measures:

- Customs duties on imports and exports; and
- Charges having equivalent effect to customs duties (CHEEs).

Article 23 also mentions "goods", a term which is not defined in the Treaty. In *Commission v Italy ((re Export Tax on Art Treasures)* [1968]), Italy levied charges on the export of its national artistic heritage. It was held that these constituted goods as "products which can be valued in money and which are capable, as such, of forming the subject of commercial transactions." In *Thompson* [1978] the term "goods" was held to cover gold and silver collectors' coins provided they were not in circulation as legal tender.

Article 25 prohibits customs duties on imports and exports:

> "Customs duties on imports and exports and charges having equivalent effect shall be prohibited between Member States. This prohibition shall also apply to customs duties of a fiscal nature."

In *Commission v Italy (re Export Tax on Art Treasures)* the Court stated that in view of its fundamental nature there could only be express exceptions to this prohibition and such exceptions would be interpreted strictly.

What are Customs Charges?
Customs charges are taxes, duties, and tariffs levied by the Member State whenever goods cross borders.

What are "charges having an equivalent effect to customs duties"?
The Treaty does not define this term but it was held by the Court in 1966 (*Germany v Commission*) to mean in this case, charges imposed on imports of agricultural products in the guise of administrative fees imposed in exchange for tasks undertaken by the authorities in the interest of, and at the request of individuals. The Court ruled that they were still unilateral measures, imposed by the state of its own volition which, regardless of their label and the means by which they were introduced, had the same discriminatory and protective effect as customs duties. In other words, the name of the charge was not important; it was the effect that mattered. Accordingly, the action by Germany was dismissed.

The *Bauhuis* case in 1977 gave the most complete definition. The Court said that:

> "any pecuniary charge—whatever its assignation and mode of application, which is levied unilaterally on goods by reason of the fact that they cross the frontier and which is not a customs duty in the strict sense, constitutes a charge with equivalent effect unless it relates to a general system of internal taxation applied systematically in accordance with the same criteria and at the same stage of marketing to domestic products alike."

Charges—no matter what they are called, or for what purpose—levied by a state solely because goods cross frontiers are charges having an equivalent effect to a customs duty, and therefore prohibited. The restrictive effect on trade between Member States of the Community that such charges engendered was prohibited.

In *Commission v Italy (re Statistical Levy)* in 1969, Italy imposed a charge on exported goods with the ostensible purpose of collecting statistical material to analyse trade patterns. The Court said that:

> "any pecuniary charge, however small, and whatever its designation and mode of application, which is imposed unilaterally on domestic and foreign goods by reason of the fact that they cross a frontier, constitutes a charge even if it is not imposed for the benefit of the state, is not discriminatory or protective in effect and if the product on which the charge is imposed is not in competition with any domestic product."

The Court's attitude was:

- The Treaty was not to be circumvented by the form in which the charge was imposed (the form of the charge is irrelevant, the effect on trade between Member States is all important);
- The prohibition applied whether the duties were discriminatory or not;
- Whether or not the product on which the charge was imposed was in competition with domestic goods; and
- There were to be no exceptions.

In the case of *Sociaal Fonds voor Diamantarbeiders v S A Brachfeld & Sons* (the *Diamond Workers* case) in 1969, Belgium levied a tax on imported diamonds which would provide social security benefits for diamond workers. Again, the Court emphasised that such charges were prohibited, irrespective of their purpose. The prohibited effect would constitute an obstacle to the free movement of goods.

What if a Fee is charged in Respect of some Service Given?

The service in question could be for a health inspection, a quality check or offloading charge. The Court accepts that a Member State is allowed to charge a fee for services provided to an importer. But such a charge is not to be levied simply because goods cross a frontier. It must be for services rendered before it is lawful.

However, the service in question must be specific and must benefit the individual importer, unlike the statistical information collected in *Commission v Italy (re Statistical Levy)* which the Court considered to be of benefit to the whole economy. The Court also took a similar approach in *Bresciani* [1976] where the question was whether an Italian charge for compulsory veterinary and public health inspections carried out on the importation of raw cowhides, was compatible with the Treaty. The submissions in *Bresciani* as well as in the *Statistical Levy* case were rejected.

If a charge is for a specific inspection, benefiting the individual importer, then it falls outside the prohibition. But there is a condition—the service rendered must be mandatory. In *Commission v Germany (re Animal Inspection Fees)* [1988] the German authorities charged fees on imports of live animals. The revenue gained was to cover the cost of inspections required to comply with Directive 81/389. Under Community law, Germany was obliged to achieve the result set out in the directive by enacting its own legislation. The inspections were mandatory.

Charges for services authorised by Community law do not constitute charges having an equivalent effect to customs duties as long as they satisfy four conditions:

(1) The fee must not exceed the actual cost of the services rendered;
(2) The service must be uniform, that is applying both to imports and domestic products;
(3) The service is prescribed by Community law—a mandatory requirement—in the general interest of the Community; and
(4) The service promotes the free movement of goods.

These conditions are very strict. If fees are charged on any inspection which is not mandatory under Community law, this constitutes an obstacle to the free movement of goods and is unlawful. Charges which cannot satisfy the conditions are classified as charges having equivalent effect to a customs duty and prohibited under Article 25 (*Commission v Germany (re Animal Inspection Fees)* [1988]).

DISCRIMINATORY INTERNAL TAXATION

This is the second of the three sets of provisions within the Treaty to guarantee the free movement of goods. These rules also relate to monetary charges levied by a Member State. Whilst Articles 23 and 25 prevent financial measures in the form of customs duties at the borders of Member States it would defeat the aim of guaranteeing the abolition of charges if a Member State could then discriminate against imported goods once they were inside the borders. Article 90 is the main Treaty provision to prevent a state from placing a fiscal disadvantage in the way of imported goods in competition with domestic goods, once they are within the state by ensuring that the internal taxation system of a Member State makes no distinction between imported and domestic products.

What distinguishes discriminatory internal taxation from a charge having equivalent effect to a customs duty is that:

• Discriminatory internal taxation is imposed on *both* imported and domestic products; and
• Charges having equivalent effect to customs duties are imposed exclusively on the imported products.

Article 90

"No Member State shall impose, directly or indirectly, on the products of other Member States any internal taxation of any kind in excess of that imposed directly or indirectly on similar domestic products.

Furthermore, no Member State shall impose on the products of other Member States any internal taxation of such a nature as to afford indirect protection to other products."

Article 90(1) deals with imported products which are so similar to domestic products that they require the same tax treatment. The important point is that the goods do not need to be identical, they only need to be similar. The term "similar" has been defined as products which are broadly in competition with one another, "with similar characteristics and meet the same needs from the point of view of the consumer" (*Commission v France (re Taxation of Spirits)* [1980]). If a product is judged to be "similar", then Article 90(1) applies (*Johnny Walker v Ministeriet for Skatter* [1986]).

If a product is not judged to be "similar", then Article 90(2) will come into play. This examines whether or not the products are likely to be in competition and assesses the protective effect of the disputed tax (*Commission v France (re Light Tobacco)* [2002]).

Article 90 does not prohibit internal taxation. Member States are free to set up systems of taxation which they consider most appropriate for each product (*Commission v France (re Levy on Reprographic Machines)* [1981]). What it does prohibit is:

- Discrimination against imported products; and
- Indirect protection of domestic projects.

Not only taxation, but the method of assessment may be discriminatory. Two different systems of taxation, one applying to domestic products and another dealing with similar imported products cannot be justified (*Bobie v HZA Aachen-Nord* [1976]). In *Commission v Ireland* [1980] the tax was charged uniformly but whereas domestic producers were allowed several weeks' grace before payment was due, importers were faced with immediate payment upon importation.

Indirect Discrimination
While direct discriminatory taxation is easy to recognise in the light of the strict prohibition in Article 90, indirect discrimination is less easy to detect. In *Humblot v Directeur des Services Fiscaux* [1985], French road tax applied tax on cars above 16cv at 5,000 FF. It was established that France did not produce any cars with an engine size of more than 16cv so the disproportionately heavy tax affected only imported goods.

Objective Justification
Even if a Member State establishes a tax system based on factors which indirectly affect imports more drastically than domestic products, the Court will allow a Member State to plead that there was some objective policy reason acceptable to the Community as a whole to justify its action. In this way, the Treaty rules are prevented from becoming too harsh. These reasons may refer to the use of raw materials, the processes employed in the production of goods or general objectives of economic policy of a Member State such as protection of the environment or development of regional policy. In the case of *Commission v France* [1987], sweet wines made in the traditional manner tended to be produced in areas of poor soil and low rainfall and where the local economy was particularly dependent on wine output. It was therefore held to be objectively justifiable to give tax concessions in order to support economically weak regions. So although there was indirect discrimination, it was excusable for France to use its tax system as a way of strengthening regional economies—provided that the concession was kept open to all products, not only to domestically produced goods.

Similarly in *Commission v Italy* in 1980, Italy imposed a tax on imported and domestic cars based on their capacity to pollute which was objectively justified on the grounds of environmental protection although in the circumstances, it imposed a heavier tax burden on imported cars than on domestic cars.

However, in the 1997 case of *Commission v Greece* concerning a Greek rule providing for a reduced rate of tax to apply to cars using "anti-pollution" technology which was not open to imports because of the practicalities of testing imported vehicles, the Court ruled that even consideration for the environment could not justify such discriminatory taxation.

The Relationship between Article 25 (Customs Charges) and Article 90 (Discriminatory Taxation)

Both Articles are complementary, yet mutually exclusive. A charge may not be examined under Articles 25 and 90 at the same time.

In principle, if a charge is imposed exclusively on imported products, it is likely to be a charge equivalent to a customs duty. If a charge is levied on both domestic and imported products in a uniform manner, it is more likely to be part of a system of internal taxation. In *Firma Steinike und Weinlig v Bundesamt für Ernährung und Fortwirtschaft* [1977], the Court held that "financial charges within a general system of internal taxation applying systematically to domestic and imported products according to the same criteria are not to be considered charges having equivalent effect".

In order to distinguish which of the two provisions a charge is likely to fall under, the Court has applied a test based on the destination of the proceeds of the charge. The case of *Fratelli Cucchi v Avez* in 1977, concerned a tax imposed on the sale of domestic and imported sugar. The proceeds of the tax provided subsidies for both Italian sugar refineries and for sugar beet producers. The Court concluded that a charge, which appeared to be part of a system of internal taxation, could be considered a charge having equivalent effect to a customs duty if the following conditions were met:

- The sole purpose of the charge must be to finance activities for the benefit of the taxed domestic product;
- The taxed product and the domestic product benefiting from the charge must be the same; and
- Any charges imposed on domestic products are made good in full.

These conditions are very strict. If all three exist, then it is a charge having equivalent effect to a customs duty prohibited under Article 25 and not part of a general system of taxation which might, if it is discriminatory be prohibited under Article 90. In both cases, unlawful charges must be repaid by the Member State.

Enforcing the Rules

Since Articles 23, 25 and 90 are directly effective, Member States may be called upon in national courts to repay any customs duties or other charges which have been found to be illegal (*Amministrazione delle Finanze dello Stato v San Giorgio* [1983]). Delictual liability may also arise with regard to breaches of Articles 25 and 90 by reason of the restrictive effect of a charge on imports from other Member States (*Just v Danish Ministry for Fiscal Affairs* [1980]).

QUANTITATIVE RESTRICTIONS AND MEASURES HAVING EQUIVALENT EFFECT TO QUANTITATIVE RESTRICTIONS

Abolishing charges on goods passing between Member States could not in themselves ensure that goods moved freely through the Community. Member States began to put up invisible barriers to trade which were not easily recognisable and as such were a more serious threat to the free movement of goods. Such measures were also capable of restricting the free movement of goods to a greater extent than charges.

A Member State may infringe these rules by failing to act as well as by acting. In *Commission v France* [1997], the Commission took action against France for failing to take all necessary and proportionate measures to prevent the free movement of fruit and vegetables from being obstructed by the actions of private individuals. Lorries transporting goods were intercepted, their loads destroyed and drivers threatened and attacked.

Contrast this with the case of *Eugen Schmidberger* [2003] where a peaceful protest on the Brenner motorway completely closed it to traffic for 30 hours. An action was brought against Austria but in this case, having weighed up the interests involved (respect for the demonstrators' rights of freedom of expression and assembly under the European Convention on Human Rights as against the free movement of goods), the Court found that as the Austrian authorities had taken steps to minimise the disturbance, a fair balance had been struck as achievement of both objectives would not have been able to have been carried out by measures less restrictive to Community trade.

Article 28 lays down the basic provision:

"Quantitative restrictions on imports and all measures having equivalent effect shall be prohibited between Member States."

Article 29 prohibits quantitative restrictions and measures having equivalent effect to quantitative restrictions (MEQRs), on exports:

"Quantitative restrictions on exports and all measures having equivalent effect shall be prohibited between Member States."

Article 30 provides for derogations: that the prohibitions in Articles 28 and 29 will not apply because of specific justifications. These derogations are allowed on several grounds so long as:

- They do not arbitrarily discriminate against goods from another Member State; and
- Are not a disguised restriction on trade between Member States.

Article 28

Article 28 prohibits two types of activity:

- Quantitative restrictions;

- Measures having an equivalent effect to quantitative restrictions.

It prevents Member States from imposing a numerical limit on the imports of a certain product in an effort to protect their own products from competition from other Member States.

Although Article 28 is addressed to Member States and concerns measures taken by them, measures taken by any public body, whether legislative, executive or judicial as well as any semi-public body which affect trade between Member States are prohibited (*Apple and Pear Development Council v K J Lewis Ltd* [1983]).

What are Quantitative Restrictions?

These were defined in the case of *Geddo v Ente Nazionale Risi* [1973], as measures which amount to a "total or partial restraint on imports, exports or goods in transit". In other words, import bans, setting of quotas and the like.

What about Measures having Equivalent Effect to Quantitative Restrictions?

These proved more difficult to define. After some pressure from Member States and the European Parliament, the Commission issued Directive 70/50 to clarify the meaning and scope of "measures having equivalent effect". Section 2 of this directive proved to be particularly valuable in setting out in a non-exhaustive list of what would be considered a "measure having equivalent effect to a quantitative restriction" with respect to national measures which apply specifically to, or affect only imported products. These are often referred to as distinctly applicable measures. Such discriminatory measures included:

- Setting minimum or maximum sale prices;
- Fixing less favourable prices for imports;
- Lowering the value of imports by increasing its costs;
- Setting conditions of payment for imports differing from those of domestic products;
- Specifying conditions for packaging, composition, identification, size, weight, etc., which would only apply to imports;
- Limiting publicity for imports compared to domestic goods; and
- Making it mandatory for importers to have an agent in the importing state.

The directive also refers to measures which are non-discriminatory or *indistinctly applicable*, that is, applying to both imports and exports but which may nevertheless restrict trade from abroad by, for example, setting disproportionately restrictive requirements on importers. The Court has developed its case law on many of these cases where it has established that the same objective can be attained by other, less burdensome means.

In *Procureur du Roi v Dassonville* [1974], the Court set out its own definition of "measures having equivalent effect" and addressed the double burden an importer may have to bear in that having already complied with domestic laws, he may also have to change his method of production or documentation to comply with the importing state's laws. Dassonville had imported a consignment of Scotch whisky to Belgium from France, without the certificate of origin required by Belgian law. This certificate proved impossible to produce and Dassonville went ahead with the transaction, even going so far as to create a home-made certificate. The company was charged under Belgian law with the criminal offence of importing goods without the requisite certificate of origin and Dassonville argued that this contravened Article 28.

The Court stated what has become known as "the *Dassonville* formula":

"all trading rules enacted by member states which are capable of hindering directly or indirectly, actually or potentially, intra-Community trade, are to be considered as measures having an effect equivalent to quantitative restrictions."

This definition includes both distinctly applicable measures affecting imports and indistinctly applicable measures affecting imports and domestic products. Thus, discrimination was not a necessary precondition for the prohibition to apply. The judgment also emphasised the effect of the restrictive practice, not the form it takes. The objectionable part of the Belgian law was that its effect hindered the free movement of goods. The Court continued:

"in the absence of a Community system guaranteeing for consumers the authenticity of a product's designation of origin, if a member state takes measures to prevent unfair practices....*those measures should be reasonable* and the means of proof required should not act as a hindrance to trade between member states." [emphasis added]

The *Dassonville* case was fundamental in dismantling many of the obstacles by which Member States were endeavouring to discriminate against imports and protect their own products in the process of which they were infringing Community law.

A similar case involving labelling was that of *Commission v Spain and Italy* [2003]. The Court held that the requirement in those countries to alter the sales name of chocolate made according to Directive 73/241 in Denmark, Ireland, Portugal, Sweden, Finland and the UK was disproportionate and infringed the principle of the free movement of goods. Appropriate labelling would have been sufficient to ensure that consumers were informed and thus protected.

In *Commission v Ireland* [1982], the Irish Goods Council conducted a campaign to promote Irish products. The Court held that the campaign was in breach of Article 28 as it intended to substitute domestic products for imports in the Irish market, the effect of which would be to restrict imports from other Member States.

Not all measures which promote domestic goods will be caught by Article 28. In *Apple and Pear Development Council* [1983], although this body was set up by the UK Government, it was financed by fees paid by domestic growers and its task was to promote the consumption of apples and pears. It brought actions against some of the fruit growers who refused to pay the charge. The actions were defended on the basis that the charges were contrary to Article 28. In its judgment, the Court stated that a Member State would be entitled to promote its own products, but that the marketing in question would be considered unlawful under Article 28 if it was intended to discourage the purchase of imported products. Competition in terms of quality is desirable, but discrimination on the grounds of nationality infringes Community law.

In *Commission v Italy* [1991], Italian public authorities had to buy Italian made cars before they could get subsidies. This measure discriminated against imports, affected trade between Member States and was thus prohibited.

In *Tasca* [1976], Tasca attempted to sell sugar above the maximum price set by the Italian authorities for both imported and domestic sugar. While national law prohibiting price increases on sugar would not of itself constitute a measure having equivalent effect (indistinctly applicable), if prices are fixed at such a low level that the sale of imports becomes more difficult or costly than the sale of domestic sugar, then the Member State would be in breach of Community law.

In *Openbaar Ministerie v Van Tiggele* [1978], criminal proceedings were brought against Van Tiggele for selling gin below the national fixed price. The fixing of a minimum price for both imported and domestic products was not in breach of Article 28, provided it did not restrict imports. However, it would be unlawful if importers were to be placed at a relative disadvantage because they could not make any profit on their products under these circumstances or because the competitive advantage conferred by lower prices is cancelled out. The Dutch law was in breach of Article 28.

After *Dassonville*, the next major development was the case of *Cassis de Dijon* (*Rewe-Zentral AG v Bundermonopolverwaltung für Branntwein*) in 1979. German law laid down a minimum alcohol content of 25 per cent for cassis—a blackcurrant liqueur—though the alcohol content of the French cassis was only 15 per cent. Although this minimum level applied both to imports and domestic goods, its effect was to exclude French cassis from the German market. This measure was challenged by German importers on the grounds that it infringed Article 28.

What emerges from the *Cassis* case are two fundamental principles of Community law. The first is the "rule of reason", whereby if there is no Community legislation on a particular topic, each Member State is free to take reasonable measures to prevent unfair trade practices. Prior to *Cassis* the emphasis had been on whether or not the measure had been discriminatory; now the rule of reason set out a non-exhaustive list of the type of measures a Member State may take, though these must be proportionate.

The second *Cassis* principle is that of mutual recognition. It states that if goods have been lawfully produced and marketed in one Member State, complying with the mandatory requirements of that State, there should be no valid reason why they should not be imported into any other Member State.

This judgment in *Cassis* built upon the foundations of *Dassonville* and meant that:

- In the absence of Community rules regarding the production and marketing of goods each Member State is free to lay down its own rules;
- Which must be in proportion to the measure taken;
- But not if these rules have the effect of hindering intra-Community trade;

- And only if these rules were mandatory—to defend consumers, protect public health, promote fair trade and the effectiveness of fiscal supervision; and
- If the goods were lawfully produced and marketed in one Member State there must be clearly justifiable reasons why they cannot be sold in another Member State.

Cassis was also important because it removed the assumption after *Dassonville* that Article 28 would only apply where discrimination between imports and domestic products could be shown and emphasised that market access was the main criterion.

In *Oosthoek's* [1982], national law restricted the distribution of free gifts in the interests of consumers. The Court stated that:

> "the possibility cannot be ruled out that to compel a producer either to adopt advertising or sales promotion schemes which differ from one Member State to another or to discontinue a scheme which he considers to be particularly effective may constitute an obstacle to imports even if the legislation in question applies to domestic products and imported products without distinction."

In *Walter Rau Lebensmittelwerke v De Smedt PVBA* [1987], the Court ruled that a Belgian requirement that margarine should be sold in cube-shaped boxes in order to distinguish it from butter was disproportionate. Consumers would be sufficiently protected by appropriate and clear labelling of the product, rather than such a method which would be likely to hinder intra-Community trade.

In *Commission v Germany (re German Beer Purity Laws)* [1987], the Court held that German law stating that the word "bier" could only be used for products brewed in accordance with the country's special laws on brewing were disproportionate in that they went far beyond what was necessary to protect public health, the ostensible reason for the German legislation.

In *Cinéthèque* [1985], French law prohibited the marketing of videos of films, both domestic and imported, during the first year of the film's release. The Court stated that the protection of cultural activities constituted a mandatory requirement.

In *Commission v United Kingdom (re Origin Marking of Retail Goods)* [1985], the Court stated that a UK requirement to protect consumers by marking all goods with their country of origin would affect trade between Member States as such marking might encourage consumers to exercise their prejudices in favour of national products and avoid Community produced goods.

In *Commission v Denmark (re Returnable Containers)* [1989], the Court held that despite special arrangements for importers as an exception to the Danish requirement for approved reusable containers, this national rule was disproportionate. The concession for limited quantities of imports was not sufficient to redeem the breach of Article 28.

On October 3, 1980, the Commission adopted a Communication concerning the consequences of the *Cassis* judgment ([1980] O.J. C256/2). It read as follows:

"Any product imported from another Member State must in principle be admitted to the territory of the importing State if it has been lawfully produced, that is, conforms to rules and processes of manufacturer that are customary and traditionally accepted in the exporting country, and is marketed in the territory of another."

Nevertheless, some cases relating to the retail sector illustrated the difficulties encountered in ascertaining whether or not a measure fell within Article 28.

In *Torfaen B.C. v B & Q plc* [1989], a retail superstore was prosecuted for violation of the Sunday Trading Act of 1950 which had the effect of reducing sales by about 10 per cent with a corresponding reduction in imports from other Member States. B & Q claimed this constituted a "measure having equivalent effect" within Article 28. After some confusion as to what constituted a "trading rule" it was held that such measures were a "legitimate part of economic and social policy" and were designed to accord with "national or regional socio-cultural characteristics". The Court held that English Sunday trading rules did not therefore breach Article 28 provided that their restrictive effect was not disproportionate to their purpose.

In *Ministère Publique v Marchandise* [1989], a Belgian law which prohibited the employment of workers in shops on Sunday afternoon was held not to be disproportionate to the socio-cultural aim pursued.

In *Stoke on Trent City Council v B & Q plc* [1992], the question of English Sunday trading rules again came before the Court. It ruled that the Sunday Trading Act was within the prohibition set out in Article 28 but that it could be allowed to stand provided its objective was justified under Community law and in proportion to the aim to be achieved.

However, the Court in *Keck and Mithouard* [1993], decided to "re-examine and clarify" its case law. Keck and Mithouard were convicted of selling goods at a loss contrary to French law. The Court stated that the *Dassonville* rule only prohibited measures that related to product characteristics and did not apply to selling arrangements, as long as the selling arrangements,

"apply to all affected traders operating within the national territory and provided that they affect in the same manner, in law and in fact, the marketing of domestic products and those from other Member States".

Member States could thus determine their own measures to regulate selling arrangements where these would have no effect on imports and would not discriminate against imported goods. They would not fall within the prohibition of Article 28. Conversely, measures which concerned the packaging of goods would fall within Article 28 since they imposed a dual burden on the importer and such measures would need to be justified.

Keck thus limited the scope of the *Dassonville* formula. Under the previous approach, selling arrangements such as restrictions on opening times fell within the prohibition of Article 28 and thus required justification under Article 30 or the *Cassis* mandatory requirements. Post-*Keck*, such selling arrangements did not come within the scope of Article 28 of the EC Treaty. Examples post-*Keck* included rules on the opening times of petrol stations *(Tankstation 'T Heukske and Boermans* [1994]), advertising bans imposed on pharmacists (*Hünermund* [1993]), requirements that baby milk only be sold in pharmacies (*Commission v Greece* [1995]) and selling potatoes at a loss (*Belgapom* [1995]).

The clarification offered by *Keck* proved to be of only limited assistance. For example what would happen in the case where the selling arrangement rules and the product characteristics rules could not be separated from one another? Such a case occurred in *Mars* [1995]. Ice-cream bars were sold with 10 per cent extra free. The product packaging itself intimated this fact through use of an eye-catching flash. German consumer protection law considered the packaging to be misleading since the "10 per cent free" advert flash on the product packaging was larger than the actual 10 per cent increase in size. The German restriction was a MHEE under Article 28 and had to be justified. The German action was held to be disproportionate.

Further problems arose over the issue of television advertising. Total bans on advertising certain products will not be considered as simply selling arrangements and will be more akin to a marketing or product requirement, which would fall within Article 28 and require justification (*De Agostini* [1997]).

In conclusion, the *Keck* clarification has been useful to a degree. Now, the vast majority of national rules that restrict where, when and how goods are to be sold do not come within the purview of Article 28. Selling arrangements only create a problem when they make it more difficult for foreign producers to sell their goods in the territory.

Exports—Article 29
Article 29 reads:

> "Quantitative restrictions on exports, and all measures having equivalent effect, shall be prohibited between Member States."

So far most of the cases considered have involved national measures on imports. Article 29 applies in much the same way as Article 28 but it refers to *exports*. The principle of a Member State's action in hindering Community trade is the same.

In *Procureur de la République Besançon v Bouhelier* [1977], a French law which necessitated quality checks on watches for exports, but no checks on watches which were to be sold in France was held to be a measure equivalent to a quantitative restriction on exports.

In *PB Groenveld* [1979], a Dutch law prohibited all domestic producers of meat products from stocking or processing horsemeat. This would avoid the risk of exporting horsemeat to countries which did not allow its sale. The Court stated that:

> "national measures which have as their specific object or effect the restriction of patterns of exports and thereby the establishment of a difference in treatment between the domestic trade of a Member State and its export trade in such a way as to provide a particular advantage for national production or for the domestic market of the State in question at the expense of the production or of trade of other Member States."

Derogations

Article 30 provides for exceptions to the fundamental rule that all obstacles to the free movement of goods between Member States should be abolished. The Court has stated that like all derogations, this list of exceptions should be interpreted strictly. It will scrutinise national rules which discriminate against goods from other Member States before it confirms derogation. It will not extend the derogations beyond those listed in Article 30. The list is exhaustive.

Article 30 reads as follows:

"The provisions of Articles 28 and 29 shall not preclude prohibitions or restrictions on imports, exports or goods in transit justified on grounds of public morality, public policy or public security; the protection of health and life of humans, animals or plants; the protection of national treasures possessing artistic, historic or archaeological value; or the protection of industrial and commercial property. Such prohibitions or restrictions shall not however, constitute a means of arbitrary discrimination or a disguised restriction on trade between Member States."

Article 30 is in two parts. The first part lists the exceptions to the prohibitions. The second part goes on to warn Member States that any derogation submitted must not be a means of arbitrary discrimination or a disguised restriction on intra-Community trade.

When a Member State claims that the measure at issue has been adopted under one of these derogations, it must establish:

• That it is necessary for the measure to be adopted—the test of necessity; and
• That the measure chosen was the least restrictive means of achieving the objective—the test of proportionality.

Arbitrary discrimination means that the measure gives advantages to the marketing of domestic products—or imports—or exports from one Member State at the expense of another (*Commission v France (re Advertising of Alcoholic Beverages)* [1980]).

Disguised restrictions are measures which are ostensibly justified under Article 30, but which have the effect of restricting the free movement of goods (*Commission v UK (re Imports of Poultry Meat)* [1982]).

Where the Community has already taken action to make sure that there are harmonising measures or standards set up in a particular area, Member States may not justify their own national rules which infringe Article 28 and restrict intra-Community trade, by pleading exemption through Article 30.

The burden of proof rests upon the Member State relying on the derogation.

Public Morality

Member States may set out what constitutes public morality in accordance with their own scales of values. However, they must not impose double standards—one to prevent the sale and marketing of domestic products and another relating only to imports.

In *R v Henn and Darby* in 1979, the defendants were charged with importing "indecent or obscene articles" into the UK from the Netherlands. They pleaded that this UK law was contrary to the free movement of goods despite the UK government's assertion that the prohibition on such imports fell within the derogation on "public morality". On the other hand in the case of *Conegate* [1986], the seizure of sex dolls was not justified under Article 30. On this occasion, the Court stated that because it was legal to manufacture these items in the UK—although it was subject to restrictions on where and to whom it might be sold—the UK itself was not in a position to restrict similar imports from abroad.

Public Policy
Under this heading a Member State must show the imports or exports in question would be a genuine and sufficiently serious threat to one of the fundamental interests of its society. In *Thompson* [1978], criminal proceedings were commenced against UK citizens who imported gold coins despite a ban on such activity. The UK's submission succeeded on the grounds of public policy.

The Court has ruled on all other cases very strictly. What has been ruled to be inapplicable to the public policy derogation are measures that seek to excuse Member State action on the grounds of:

- Avoidance of civil unrest which the national authorities were well able to cope with—*Cullet v Centre Leclerc* [1985];
- Restriction of criminal behaviour—*Prantl* [1984]; and
- Protection of consumers—*Kohl v Ringelhan* [1984].

Public Security
In *Campus Oil Ltd v Minister for Industry and Energy* [1984], the Irish government succeeded before the Court with its requirement that importers buy one-third of what they needed from the state-owned oil refinery on the grounds that without this revenue, the refinery would have to close down. This would mean that Ireland would have no source of oil to supply key national institutions and services in the event of a national crisis.

Protection of the Health and Life of Humans, Animals and Plants
The Court considers that the "health and life of humans ranks first among the interests protected" by Article 30 (*De Peijper* [1975]). In *Commission v UK (re UHT Milk)* [1983], the Court accepted a justification that an import licence system was necessary to regulate the heat treatment of imported milk and to trace the origins of infected milk, but re-treating and re-packaging imported milk was an unjustified restriction on trade because milk from other Member States was already subject to similar controls before export. This requirement was simply a disguised restriction on intra-Community trade.

In *R v Royal Pharmaceutical Society Ex p. API* [1989], the code of ethics laid down by the pharmacists' professional body did not allow a pharmacist to substitute, except in an emergency, any other medicine for that specifically named in a doctor's prescription, even where the pharmacist believed that the effect and quality of the substitute were identical. The Court found this rule discriminated against imports but accepted the UK's justification as being on the grounds of public health.

The protection of the health and life of animals was successfully pleaded in *Bluhme* [1998], where, in order to protect the Læsø Brown Bee, the Court ruled that a Danish law prohibiting the importation of other live bees to the island of Læsø was justified.

Restrictions on the sale of extremely strong alcohol may also be accepted in light of the dangers posed to society (*Ahokainen and Leppik* [2007]).

Protection of National Treasures Possessing Artistic, Historic or Archaeological Value

Member States are entitled to determine the value of their national treasures possessing artistic, historic or archaeological value and may determine restrictions on their import. However, any protection afforded may not justify charges (*Commission v Italy (First Art Treasures Case)* [1968]).

In the mid-1990s, legislation was adopted to ensure that the free movement of goods would not increase illegal exports of such national treasures (Directive 93/7 on the Return of Cultural Objects Unlawfully Removed from the Territory of a Member State and Regulation 3911/92 on the Control of the Export of Cultural Goods).

Protection of Industrial and Commercial Property

This ground of derogation is controversial in that it essentially serves private aims as opposed to public objectives, in that it operates to protect intellectual property holders. The Court of Justice has been circumspect in restricting the right to utilise this derogation. Since intellectual property protection has the potential to undermine the single market, through partitioning of national markets, the Court has made a fundamental distinction between the existence and exercise of the right. Thus, intellectual property owners may not exercise their rights where such action would threaten the coherency of the internal market. Secondly, the Court has confirmed that intellectual property rights are subject to the concept of European exhaustion; that is once the owner has placed the goods on the single market, he/she cannot prevent further EU trade in the goods.

---

10. FREE MOVEMENT OF WORKERS

The free movement of workers constitutes one of the cornerstones of the internal market. An extensive system of Treaty provisions, secondary legislation and the case law of the Court has provided for a system of employment rights throughout the Community prohibiting national legislation which might place other Community nationals at a disadvantage when they seek to exercise their right of free movement. The basic principle covering these rights is that of non-discrimination of persons from other Member States on the grounds of nationality as set out in Article 12. This principle is incorporated within all the other provisions in this area either through the Treaty, in the secondary legislation or through the case law of the Court.

Among the provisions promoting free movement of workers are the following:

- Article 17 establishes citizenship of the European Union. Every person holding the nationality of a Member State is a citizen of the Union. Citizenship of the Union complements and does not replace national citizenship. Under Article 18, every Union citizen has the right to move and reside freely within the territory of the Member States, subject to the limitations and conditions laid down in the Treaty and by the secondary legislation adopted to give effect to these provisions.
- Article 39 defines what is meant by free movement of workers. This is considered in detail below.
- Article 40 relates to the implementation of Article 39 by setting out the legislative manner in which the goal of free movement may be achieved. It relates to close co-operation between national employment services, abolishing restrictions and by setting up appropriate machinery "to bring offers of employment into touch with applications for employment and to facilitate the achievement of a balance between supply and demand in the employment market in such a way as to avoid serious threats to the standard of living and level of employment in the various regions and industries".
- Article 41 provides for the exchange of young workers.
- Article 42 relates to social security in relation to the free movement of workers.
- Article 12 provides a general prohibition of discrimination on the grounds of nationality.
- The Treaty of Amsterdam introduced a new Article 13 to promote action to combat discrimination based on sex, racial or ethnic origin, religion or belief, disability, age or sexual orientation (*see also* Chapter 13, Equal Treatment).
- Several major pieces of secondary legislation also facilitated those falling within their personal scope to exercise their right of free movement. Unfortunately, the fact that there was such a volume of legislation governing this area meant that citizens were often unsure of their exact rights under the Treaty and the secondary legislation, such that they were discouraged from actually exercising these rights. Therefore, the Commission introduced Directive 2004/38 to consolidate the law in this area. The directive broadly repeals the secondary legislation, however a number of provisions of the old law are still in force, in particular certain provisions of Regulation 1612/68.

Article 39 sets out that:

> "(1) Freedom of movement for workers shall be secured within the Community.
> (2) Such freedom of movement shall entail the abolition of any discrimination based on nationality between workers of the Member States as regards employment, remuneration and other conditions of work and employment.

(3) It shall entail the rights, subject to limitations justified on grounds of public policy, public security or public health—

(a) to accept offers of employment actually made;

(b) to move freely within the territory of Member States for this purpose;

(c) to stay in a Member State for the purpose of employment in accordance with the provisions governing the employment of nationals of that State laid down by law, regulation or administrative action;

to remain in the territory of a Member State after having been employed in that State, subject to conditions which shall be embodied in implementing regulations to be drawn up by the Commission.

(4) The provisions of this Article shall not apply to employment in the public sector."

Article 39 is directly effective (*Royer* [1977]), both vertically against a Member State and horizontally, against employers (*Clean Car Autoservice* [1998]).

Free movement and its associated Community rights are not unconditional. Some restrictions apply:

- A worker must exercise his Community right to free movement in order to benefit from employment rights in another Member State. Community rights do not apply if a worker moves from one region of his home country to another. In such cases, the relevant national law applies (*R v Saunders* [1979] and *Morson and Jhabjan* [1982]).
- Member States may also restrict access to employment of other Member State nationals on the grounds of public policy, public security and public health (Article 39(3) and Directive 2004/38).
- Member States may reserve access to employment in the public service to their own nationals under certain conditions (Article 39(4)).

The Community protection afforded also applies to those who move from one Member State to another to seek work. In *R v IAT Ex p. Antonissen* in 1991, a Belgian national had entered the UK but more than six months later he had still not succeeded in finding a job. The Court said that deportation would be allowed where an individual had been in a Member State for more than six months, unless he could produce evidence that he was still seeking work and had a genuine chance of being offered employment. This principle now finds expression in Article 14(4) of Directive 2004/38.

All the rights under Article 39 and its associated secondary legislation are granted to workers and their families. The families' rights depend on their relationships with the worker and are thus described as parasitic rights.

WHAT IS A WORKER?

Neither Article 39 nor the secondary legislation defines the term "worker". In clarifying its scope, the Court has emphasised that "worker" must have a Community meaning inasmuch as it defines the scope of one of the fundamental freedoms of the Community. It must thus be interpreted widely

(*Bettray v Staatssecretaris van Justitie* [1989]). In this and in other cases, the Court further interpreted the term "worker". The criteria for qualifying as a worker within the meaning of Article 39 are that a person performs services of some economic value for and under the direction of another person, in return for which he/she receives remuneration (*Lawrie Blum* [1986]).

* *Hoekstra v BBDA* [1964], although having lost her job in the Netherlands, Mrs Hoekstra was capable of taking another. The Court ruled that the term "worker" applied not exclusively to one who is currently employed but to a person "who is likely to remain in the territory of a Member State after having been employed in that state".
* *Levin* [1982], Mrs Levin was a part-time chambermaid working for wages below the minimum subsistence considered necessary in the Netherlands. As long as the work met the economic activity criterion, it did not matter whether or not the individual could support themselves on the money they earned.
* *Lawrie-Blum* [1986], Miss Lawrie-Blum was a trainee teacher working under supervision but receiving remuneration for conducting classes.
* *Kempf* [1986], Mr Kempf was a part-time music teacher who gave lessons for 12 hours a week. The Court stated that it did not matter whether the money used to supplement the income was from the individual's private means or from public funds.
* *Steymann* [1988], Mr Steymann was a member of a religious commune who undertook plumbing and general household duties for board, lodgings and pocket money but not a formal wage. The outside work which he also undertook—a necessary part of the commune's self-sufficiency—was held to be a genuine and effective economic activity.
* *URSAFF v Hostellerie le Manoir* [1991], the term "worker" was held to cover students on courses which required practical work experience in another Member State.
* *Raulin* [1992], the concept of "a worker" included a person who worked occasionally under a contract with no fixed hours but according to the needs of an employer.
* *CPM Meeusen v Hoofddirectie Van De Informatie Beheer Groep* [1999], a person related by marriage to the director and sole shareholder of the company may be classified as a "worker" if he/she pursues an effective and genuine economic activity.

But in *Bettray*, the Court refused to accept that an individual who was working in a drug rehabilitation scheme was in fact a worker, because no real and genuine economic activity was taking place.

The Court has continued to abide by the three-part Community definition of a worker as set out in *Lawrie-Blum* (above). This is that the individual concerned:

* Performs a service of economic value;
* For and under the direction of another person; and
* Receives payment.

ACCESS TO EMPLOYMENT

Regulation 1612/68 (as amended) provides that any national of a Member State, irrespective of his residence, has the right to take up activity as an employed person and to pursue this activity within the territory of another Member State in accordance with the provisions laid down governing the employment of nationals of that Member State. In particular, he must have the right to take up any available employment in the host Member State under the same conditions as those allowed to nationals of that state.

According to Directive 2004/38, his/her spouse, registered partner (if national law treats such relationships as equivalent to marriage) and direct descendants who are under the age of 21 or dependent on the worker (including children of the spouse/partner), have the right to reside and to take up any employment throughout the territory of that same state even if they are not nationals of any Member State of the Union (Article 23 of Directive 2004/38). In addition, dependent relatives in the ascending line of the worker and his spouse/partner, have the right to live with the worker/self-employed person. The worker is entitled to all the housing rights and benefits accorded to national workers. His children are entitled to be admitted to general education, apprenticeship and vocational training courses under the same conditions as nationals of the host Member State. The worker is entitled to the same social and tax advantages and access to the same training in vocational schools and retraining centres as a national worker. Any collective or individual agreement regarding eligibility for employment, remuneration and other conditions of work or dismissal is null and void to the extent that it discriminates against workers who are nationals of another Member State.

The regulation therefore gives valuable rights to workers, in particular concerning:

* Eligibility *for employment*;
* Equality of treatment *within employment*; and
* Rights for the families of those who *are employed*.

The material scope of the main sections of the regulation are set out below.

Eligibility for Employment
Articles 1 to 6 of the regulation allows migrant workers from another Member State the right to take up employment under the same conditions as the host state's nationals. This means that Member States must not specify discriminatory employment policies and companies must not operate such practices. In particular, they cannot discriminate in methods of recruitment, advertising vacancies or setting eligibility standards to apply for employment. However, Article 3(1) allows Member States to impose conditions "relating to linguistic knowledge required by reason of the nature of the post to be filled" (*Groener* [1989]). Article 4 prohibits quota systems setting out what percentage of foreign nationals may be employed (*Commission v France (Re French Merchant Seamen)* [1974]) and *Bosman* [1995]. Article 5 requires that similar assistance must be extended to nationals of other Member States in finding employment as is given to national workers.

Equality of Treatment within Employment

Article 7(1) of the regulation provides that workers from another Member State must not be treated differently from national workers—especially regarding payment of wages or salary, dismissal and reinstatement, or re-employment if he/she becomes unemployed. Any discriminatory practices will be prohibited unless they can be justified under Article 39(4) of the Treaty (*Schöning-Kougebetopoulou v Freie und Hansestadt Hamburg* [1998]).

Social and Tax Advantages

Article 7(2) of the regulation lays down that there should be no discrimination in social and tax advantages for workers. This covers matters such as a lower separation allowance for workers from another Member State and includes public service workers (*Sotgiu v Deutsche Bundespost* [1974]). This prohibition on discrimination applies even when these advantages are not related to a contract of employment—such as a war pension in *Even* [1979] and may remain even if the worker dies so that his family can benefit—such as concessionary cards for rail travel (*Cristini* [1975]). It does not cover social security benefits to which migrant workers are entitled only if they contribute to a social security scheme in a host Member State (*Frilli v Belgium* [1972]).

- In *Reina* [1982], migrant workers were held to be entitled to a special discretionary childbirth loan which was until then payable only to German nationals.
- In *Castelli* [1984], a payment made to all old people in Belgium but not to an Italian widow living with her retired son in Belgium, was also considered unlawful.
- In *Bernini* [1992], a study grant was allowed to a dependent child of a migrant worker under the same conditions as those applicable to children of national workers.
- In *Scrivner* [1985], a minimum income allowance was allowed to members of the family of an unemployed worker.
- In *Commission v Luxembourg* [2002], a Luxembourg law providing for a guaranteed minimum income, but paid only to individuals who had lived in Luxembourg for at least five of the previous 20 years before application was held to be indirectly discriminatory against nationals of other Member States.

Vocational Training

Article 7(3) of Regulation 1612/68 concerns vocational training. In *Brown v Secretary of State for Scotland* [1988], the applicant had obtained sponsorship from a UK company prior to taking up a university place. He then applied for a grant which was refused. The Court found that the course was not "vocational training" within the meaning of Article 7(3) though it would constitute a social and tax advantage under Article 7(2). This in turn was only available to workers fulfilling the criteria in *Lawrie-Blum*. The Court decided that Brown was not entitled to a grant despite his status of a worker because he "acquired that status exclusively as a result of his being accepted for admission to undertake the studies in question".

However, in *Lair* [1988], the applicant was a French national who had worked in Germany for five years and had requested a similar grant from the German government. Again this was held not to be vocational training under Article 7(3) but because she had been a worker, she was entitled to social and tax advantages under Article 7(2) even if she was involuntarily unemployed. However, the Court stated that a migrant worker who gave up a job to pursue further training would only be eligible for a grant when there was a close link between the work and the subject studied.

Workers' Families

Article 2(2) of Directive 2004/38 defines what is meant by "members of a worker's family" for the purpose of deciding who will be allowed to migrate with the worker to the host state. These are:

- A worker's spouse/partner (where national law treats registered partnerships and marriage as equivalent) and descendants who are under the age of 21 or are dependants, including those of the spouse/partner; and
- Dependant relatives in the ascending line of the worker and his/her spouse/partner.

In *Lebon* [1987], it was established that even if an adult child is over 21, if he or she is still dependant, then they are still regarded in law as members of the family and are entitled to claim Community family rights. The dependency is as a result of a factual situation, not derived from the national legislation of a host Member State.

The extension of the family member rights to include partners in addition to spouses is a recognition of progressive case law developments in the area (*Reed* [1986]), which in themselves explicitly acknowledged the immense societal changes occurring within the European Union. If a married couple separates at any time, spouse's rights do not come to an end until they are divorced (*Diatta* [1985]). By virtue of Directive 2004/38, it is submitted that this right extends to partners in a relationship analogous to marriage. In the case of divorce or termination of partnership, the family member is now explicitly granted the right to remain in the host territory (Article 13 of the directive). The directive does however make a distinction between family members who are EU nationals and those who have third country nationality. For ex-partners/spouses who possess a third country nationality right to reside will depend upon the existence of a number of factors, such as, sufficient length of the relationship, the custody and access situation as regards children of the marriage/relationship and the prior existence of "particularly difficult circumstances" such as domestic violence.

Members of a worker's family are entitled to migrate with the worker regardless of their own nationality—though of course the worker must be the national of another Member State. Family rights under Directive 2004/38 depend entirely on whether the worker has exercised his/her right to cross-border movement (*Morson and Jhabjan v the Netherlands* [1982]).

Article 12 of Regulation 1612/68 provides that children are entitled to non-discriminatory access not only to general educational, apprenticeship and vocational training courses but also to grants and loans (*Casagrande* [1974]).

Regulation 1612/68 provides other equal treatment rights for migrant workers such as Trade Union rights and housing rights (Articles 8 and 9).

RIGHT TO REMAIN

Article 39(3)(d) of the EC Treaty and Chapter IV of Directive 2004/38 outline the right of permanent residence. Union citizens and family members gain the right of permanent residence where they have legally resided in the host state for a continuous period of five years (Article 16(1) and (2) of the Directive). Temporary absences for less than six months or longer absences of up to a year listed in subsection (3) of Article 16 will not invalidate the claim for permanent residency. However, an absence of more than two years will revoke the right of permanent residency (Article 16(4)).

Article 17 of Directive 2004/38 grants the right of permanent residency to:

- Retired workers/self-employed persons;
- Workers/self-employed persons who are permanently incapacitated and unable to work; and
- Frontier workers/self-employed persons.

The right is only granted when the following conditions are satisfied:

(1) Retired workers/self-employed persons. The individual has worked in the host Member State for the last 12 months, lived there for the previous three years and has now retired.

(2) Incapacitated workers/self-employed persons. The individual has lived in the host Member State for the previous two years and has stopped working because of permanent incapacity. Where the incapacity occurred as a result of an occupational disease or accident, the two year rule is inapplicable.

(3) Frontier workers/self-employed persons. The individual worker has lived and worked in the host state for three years, but works in another Member State while continuing to live in the first Member State.

In all cases, the family of the worker/self-employed person is allowed to stay permanently, even after the death or departure of the worker/self-employed individual (Article 12 of Directive 2004/38). In the case of third country nationality family members, the Article requires that that family member must have lived in the host state for at least one year prior to death. The family is also entitled to equal treatment as stated in Regulation 1612/68 as per social and tax advantages. Article 13 of Directive 2004/38 provides for the right of residence in the case of divorce, annulment and termination of marriage or registered partnership.

RIGHT OF EXIT, ENTRY AND RESIDENCE

The right of entry to and residence in another Member State and the right to leave one's own state are of fundamental importance not just as regards employment and self-employment, but are also essential in guaranteeing the other freedoms of the Treaty, most notably the citizenship rights of Articles

17 and 18 of the EC Treaty. Thus, in order to reflect the significant developments that have taken place in the concept of Union citizenship, the provisions on exit, entry and residence for workers contained in Directive 68/360 were significantly updated and extended to encompass all Union citizens, by virtue of Directive 2004/38.

Directive 2004/38 enumerates the following autonomous rights for Union citizens, and their family members:

- To leave the territory of a Member State and to enter another Member State, subject to possession of a passport or valid identity card (Article 4). Union citizens must be granted or be able to renew a passport or identity card. Non-EU family members must posses a valid passport.
- To enter another Member State upon presentation of a valid identity card or passport (Article 5). Family members can enter with a valid passport. The host Member State may require an entry visa for third country national family members.
- To reside in the territory of the host Member State for up to three months without any conditions or formalities other than those applicable to possession of a valid passport or identity card, as applicable (Article 6).
- To reside in the territory of the host Member State beyond three months where one of the following criteria is satisfied:

  The Union citizen is a worker or self-employed person in the host Member State.

  The Union citizen and family members are not a burden on the social assistance system of the host Member State; that is they have "sufficient resources".

  The Union citizen is enrolled on a course of study at a recognised educational establishment, has comprehensive sickness insurance and has sufficient resources to prevent him/her becoming a burden on the social assistance system of the host Member State.

In the case of residence beyond three months, the directive permits Member States to impose certain registration formalities upon the Union citizen and his/her family members (Articles 8 and 9). In particular, the host Member State must provide for registration to be open for at least three months after arrival. Thereupon, a registration certificate must be issued, in the situation where the Union citizen presents a valid identity card or passport and proof of either employment/self-employment, proof of sufficient resources and appropriate sickness insurance, or proof of enrolment on an approved course of study, sufficient resources and appropriate sickness insurance. In the case of EU national family members, a residence certificate will be issued upon presentation of a valid identity card or passport and documentary evidence of the relevant family relationship. Non-EU national family members must comply with the requirements of Articles 9-11. The third county family member must apply for a residence card, which will be issued upon presentation of the family member's passport, official evidence of the family relationship and the registration certificate of the Union citizen. The residence card must be valid for at least five years. A failure to comply with formalities regarding entry and residence cannot justify a deportation order. Any such applicable sanctions for non-compliance must be non-discriminatory and proportionate (Articles 8(2) and 9(3) of Directive 2004/38; *R v Pieck* [1980]; *Royer* [1977]; *Watson and Belmann* [1976]).

EXCEPTIONS TO THE FREE MOVEMENT OF WORKERS

Article 39(3) and Directive 2004/38

As well as requiring a worker to *exercise* the right to free movement between Member States before claiming the benefit of Community rights, exceptions allowing a Member State to restrict this right arise with the derogations set out in Article 39(3) in conjunction with Directive 2004/38. These derogations are limited to public policy, public security and public health. The directive covers expulsion from the territory of a host Member State and sets out procedural safeguards which must be followed by public authorities if they seek to exclude non-nationals.

The derogations under Article 39(3) only apply when a Member State considers the exclusion of an individual from its territory, but they cannot be used to discriminate against him regarding his employment once the individual has lawfully entered the country.

Public Policy and Public Security

These derogations must be:

- Interpreted strictly (*Van Duyn* [1974]);
- Proportionate to the objective pursued (Article 27(2) of Directive 2004/38; *Bond Van Adverteerders* [1988]); and
- Based exclusively on the personal conduct of the person involved. Previous criminal convictions are not in themselves sufficient grounds for taking any measures, such as deportation (Article 27(2) of Directive 2004/38).

In *Bonsignore* [1975], an Italian working in Germany accidentally shot and killed his brother. This did not carry a prison sentence but Bonsignore was convicted of possession of an unlicensed gun and received a deportation order as a general preventative measure to deter other immigrants from committing similar offences. The Court stated that such measures must be based solely on the personal conduct of the person concerned.

In *Bouchereau* [1977], a Frenchman working in Britain was recommended for deportation after he had twice been convicted of drug offences. Again, the Court looked strictly at the UK's reasons for deportation and stated that the public policy derogation may only be invoked where there is a genuine, sufficiently serious and present threat to one of the fundamental interests of society.

In *Adoui and Cornuaille* [1982], two French prostitutes appealed against the Belgian authorities' refusal to grant them a residence permit, despite prostitution not being an offence in Belgium. The Court considered that Member States may only justify restrictions on the admission to, or residence within, its territory on nationals of another Member State if it adopted, with respect to the same conduct on the part of its own nationals, repressive measures or other genuine and effective measures intended to combat such conduct.

In *Mary Carpenter* [2002], a Philippine national married to a UK citizen faced deportation for outstaying her original leave to enter the country. The Court held that the decision to deport did not strike a fair balance between the competing interests of respect for family life and the maintenance of public order and public safety. Ms Carpenter's personal conduct had never been the subject of complaint, the marriage was genuine and in those circumstances, the Court considered that deporting her would be an infringement of a right that was not proportionate to the objective pursued. By virtue of Article 28 of Directive 2004/38, Member States, when deciding whether to expel an individual must now explicitly take into account factors such as length of residence, age, health, family and economic factors, the extent of integration into the culture of the host Member State and links with the home Member State. Further, individuals who have acquired permanent residence as well as minor members of the family cannot be expelled.

In *Calfa* [1999], an Italian tourist was expelled from Greece for possession of drugs. Greek law provided for a lifetime expulsion from Greek territory. The Court held that such a measure was disproportionate. This situation is now covered by Article 32 of Directive 2004/38. Under that Article, expulsion decisions must be reviewed after three years. The Court has also confirmed that Member States are now entitled to impose geographical restrictions on movement as an alternative to a total ban (*Olazabal* [2002]).

Public Health

Derogation from the principles of free movement on the grounds of public health may only be invoked to refuse entry or residence for the first time, since the Member State cannot rely on public health restrictions after three months have elapsed from the date of lawful arrival. However, Member States are entitled to subject migrants to medical inspections at the point of arrival. Such examinations must be free. Under the new rules of Directive 2004/38, the only diseases which justify restrictions are those with epidemic potential according to the World Health Organisation or those infectious or contagious parasitic diseases which are subject to national law controls (Article 29 of Directive 2004/38). The list is much narrower than the old law under Directive 64/221. In particular, HIV/AIDS is no longer a justifiable reason for non-admittance or deportation.

The Public Service Exception

Under Article 39(4), Member States may deny or restrict access to employment in the public services to nationals from other Member States. Because of the potential for Member States lawfully to extend preference to their own nationals and thereby discriminate against other Community nationals by classifying a wide variety of jobs as those within the public service, the Court stated that this exception should be interpreted strictly.

In *Sotgiu v Deutsche Bundespost* [1974], the Court said:

- Article 39(4) only applied to certain activities connected with the exercise of official authority.

- Since the employees concerned worked for branches of the government of the Member States, the legal designations of the jobs could easily be varied by the Member States themselves. These designations should therefore be set by the Court to prevent discrimination against nationals from other Member States.
- Article 39(4) only applied to access to employment, not to conditions of work, once a person had been employed. If a person was sufficiently loyal or trustworthy to be admitted to such employment in the first place, there were no grounds for paying them less or treating them differently because of their nationality.

In *Commission v Belgium (No. 1)* [1980], the Court reiterated that like all derogations, the public service exception must be interpreted narrowly and uniformly, with a Community meaning. It continued, "for a state to justify excluding non-nationals the post in question must require a special relationship of allegiance to the state and the reciprocity of rights and duties which formed the foundation of the bond of nationality."

The requirement for such posts to possess such allegiance and to depend upon the bond of nationality was two-fold:

(1) The posts must involve participation in the exercise of powers conferred by public law; and
(2) They must entail duties designed to safeguard the general interests of the state.

The approach taken was functional—the nature and character of the posts were important rather than their titles.

In 1988 the Commission published a document setting out some guidance on employment which it considered would not fall within the exception ([1988] O.J. C72/2). These covered posts in public health services, teaching in state schools, research for non-military purposes and public bodies responsible for administering commercial services. What would continue to be within the public service exception would be members of the armed forces, police and judiciary. There has obviously been tension in this area of law. Member States believe this is an area where a state should be able to exercise its full sovereignty and employ who they wish to serve the state without having to abide by Community rules of non-discrimination. The Commission has attempted to balance this understandable desire by setting out jobs which are security sensitive as opposed to those which are not.

In *Scholz* [1994], it was stated that "public service would be taken into account" for Ms Scholz's application for canteen work in Italy. Although she relied on her previous experience in the German public sector, the Italian authorities stated that this must be public service in Italy. This discrimination was held to be unlawful as the job itself did not warrant it.

In the case of *Colgan* [1997], restrictions imposed on entry to the Civil Service in Northern Ireland as a management trainee were held to be illegal, disproportionate and not justified by Article 39(4).

Procedural Safeguards

Directive 2004/38 also provides for procedural rights and safeguards which Member States must provide, especially if they seek to exclude an individual on the grounds of public policy, public security or public health:

- An individual should be notified in writing of any decision to expel/restrict movement under Article 27. Such notification must be comprehensible to the individual concerned and must outline precisely and in full, the reasons for the expulsion/restriction, unless this would threaten state security (Article 30 of the Directive. This Article codifies the rights expressed in *Rutili* [1975]);
- In the case of expulsion, the Member State must outline the time limit by which the person must leave the territory. The Member State must allow a period of at least one month, except in emergency situations (Article 30(3)).
- Individuals must be granted access to judicial or administrative avenues of redress, in order to appeal against the decision to expel or restrict free movement (Article 31 of the directive; *Santillo* [1980] and *Gallagher* [1994]). This provision preserves national procedural autonomy.
- Where the individual appeals against the expulsion decision and applies for a suspension of that decision, the Member State must not remove the individual, except where the expulsion order is based on a previous judicial decision, the individual has already had access to judicial review, or public security requires his/her removal. Article 31(2) of Directive 2004/38.

---

11. FREEDOM OF ESTABLISHMENT AND THE RIGHT TO SUPPLY AND RECEIVE SERVICES

Freedom of establishment and the provision and receipt of services are usually considered together because the right of establishment allows Member State nationals to set up business as self-employed persons in another Member State. It allows them to take up and pursue activities in a host Member State without discrimination on the grounds of nationality. These two rights, however, are not identical. Article 49 relating to services gives a temporary right lasting only as long as the services are provided and only if the provisions in Article 43 on the right of establishment, a *permanent* right, do not apply (*Gebhard* [1995]). This dichotomy between permanent and temporary rights determines the extent to which the host and home State are entitled to regulate the behaviour of the provider of the service. These rights apply both to natural persons (individuals) and legal persons (companies). Article 48 applies the same rights to companies formed under the law of one of the Member States, with their registered or head office within the Community. This freedom also covers the right of so-called "secondary establishment" in another Member State, meaning the right to set up a branch or subsidiary of an existing firm or company in another state.

Some Treaty provisions relating to the freedom of establishment are similar to those already set out for workers, for example:

- Article 45 of the Treaty exempts any activities which are connected, even on an occasional basis, with the exercise of official authority (*Reyners* [1974]). This is similar to the public service exception for workers in Article 39(4).
- There is also a right to remain after retirement for individuals who have established themselves in business with their families under Directive 75/34.
- The right of establishment and the right to provide (and receive) services are not absolute. Article 46(1) provides for derogations on the grounds of public policy, public security and public health which are elaborated in Directive 2004/38 above (*Calfa* [1999]).
- Directive 2004/38 covers rights for self-employed persons and their families to enter and leave the host state for the purpose of establishing themselves or providing or receiving services.
- There is no exact equivalent to Regulation 1612/68 which means there are no "social and tax advantages" as there would have been under Article 7(2) of that regulation.
- Article 43 has direct effect (*Reyners* [1974]) as does Article 49 (*Van Binsbergen* [1974]).
- Nationals of a third country, although residing lawfully in a Member State, may not rely on the Treaty provisions to establish themselves in another Member State (*Razanatsimba* [1977]). Similarly, the right to provide services is limited to EU citizens already established in a Member State.
- Similar to the case of *Saunders* concerning the free movement of workers, provisions on the freedom of establishment do not apply to situations which are internal to one Member State (*Jagerskiold* [1999]).

THE RIGHT OF ESTABLISHMENT

Article 43 provides that:

> "Within the framework of the provisions set out below, restrictions on the freedom of establishment of nationals of a Member State in the territory of another Member State shall be prohibited. Such prohibition shall also apply to restrictions on the setting up of agencies, branches or subsidiaries by nationals of any Member State established in the territory of any Member State.
>
> Freedom of establishment shall include the right to take up and pursue activities as self-employed persons and to set up and manage undertakings, in particular companies or firms within the meaning of the second paragraph of Article 48, under the conditions laid down for its own nationals by the law of the country where such establishment is effected, subject to the provisions of the Chapter relating to capital."

Article 48 provides that:

> "Companies or firms formed in accordance with the law of a Member State and having their registered office, central administration or

principal place of business within the Community shall, for the purposes of this Chapter, be treated in the same way as natural persons who are nationals of Member States.

'Companies or firms' means companies or firms constituted under civil or commercial law, including co-operative societies, and other legal persons governed by public or private law, save for those which are non-profit-making."

The Community has taken a two-pronged approach to eliminate barriers to the freedom of establishment and the provision of services:

(1) Harmonisation of Professional Qualifications

The Treaty sets out that in order to make it easier for persons to take up and pursue activities as self-employed persons, the Community would:

- Take steps to carry out a programme of secondary legislation which would ensure the mutual recognition of "diplomas, certificates and other evidence of formal qualifications"(Article 47(1)); and
- Co-ordinate national requirements governing the pursuit of non-wage-earning activities (Article 47(2)).

General programmes for abolition of discriminatory measures both in establishment and in services were drawn up in 1961 to provide for a wide range of directives intended to facilitate access by abolishing restrictions within the various sectors of the economy.

Originally, the mutual recognition system developed on a piecemeal, sector by sector basis, with architects, dentists and doctors proving to be the simplest professions to regulate and gain agreement upon. This system provided an almost cast-iron guarantee to the holder of the qualification that he/she would be entitled to practice in the host state. However, the difficulty with this approach was that it took an inordinate length of time to gain agreement between the Member States and in certain fields agreement could not be reached. Thus, by 1985 it was clear to the Commission that a new approach was required.

This new approach was more decentralised and inclusive. Directive 89/48 (Mutual Recognition of Diplomas) covered the mutual recognition of diplomas without harmonisation, but included a safeguard requiring an adaptation period in a host Member State or aptitude tests. Those who benefited from the provisions of the directive were those who could show:

- Possession of a diploma indicating that the holder has the professional qualifications required for the taking up or pursuit of a regulated profession in one of the Member States in a self-employed capacity or as an employed person;
- Completion of a post-secondary course of at least three years' duration, or of an equivalent duration part-time, at a university or establishment of higher education or another establishment of similar level; and
- Where appropriate, that the holder of the diploma has successfully completed the professional training required in addition to the post-secondary course.

Directive 92/51 was adopted dealing with areas of professional education and training but which did not fall within Directive 89/48 as the persons involved had not completed diplomas or training for three years. As with the former directive the host state may require the diploma holder to complete an adaptation period of not more than three years or to take an aptitude test.

Directive 93/16 was adopted to facilitate the free movement of doctors and the mutual recognition of their formal qualifications and diplomas and covers the knowledge, understanding and experience that a doctor had gained during his training period.

With particular regard to the difficulties encountered by lawyers who had to undergo an aptitude test, Directive 98/5 was adopted to make it easier for lawyers to practise in other Member States. Not all Member States enthusiastically took on board the requirement to enact this into domestic law. In *Commission v France (re Lawyers)* [2002] and *Commission v Ireland* [2002] the Court held that in failing to implement the provisions of the directive, both France and Ireland fell short of their obligations under the Treaty.

Directive 2005/36 modernises, liberalises and consolidates the law surrounding recognition of professional qualifications. The Member States must introduce national law to give effect to the directive by 20th October 2007.

(2) Case law on the Principle of Non-discrimination

Because there is no equivalent to Regulation 1612/68, and so no "social or tax advantages" the Court has construed Article 43 in such a way as to outlaw national measures which give certain social or tax advantages to nationals (*CPM Meeusen v Hoofddirectie Van De Informatie Beheer Groep* [1999]), or to companies having their principal establishment in that Member State (*ICI v Colmer* [1998]), and which discriminate directly or indirectly against non-national, natural or legal persons. Similar case law has excluded discrimination with regard to the provision of services.

The Court has stated that the prohibition of discrimination is concerned with the rules relating to the various facilities which are needed in order to pursue an occupation. So by applying the principle of non-discrimination where harmonisation has not taken place in a particular profession, it has been possible to invoke Articles 12, 43 and 49 to challenge traditional rules which discriminate against persons or companies from other Member States.

Both direct and indirect discrimination are prohibited. The Court has not hesitated to invoke Article 12 to strike down national rules either in the form of discriminatory nationality or residence requirements (*Steinhauser v City of Biarritz* [1985] and *Commission v Italy (re Housing Aid)* [1988]).

The case law of the Court has also clarified the qualifications required for professionals to be able to practise in other Member States:

- If a person has already obtained what was recognised, professionally and academically as an equivalent qualification and had satisfied the necessary training requirements, there should be no obstacle to his admission to a professional body in another Member State (*Thieffry v Conseil de l'Ordre des Avocats à la Cour de Paris* [1977]).

- In *Commission v Luxembourg (re Access to the Medical Profession)* [1992], the Court ruled that formalities necessary to become a member of a professional body must fulfil four criteria in order to be justified:
  (a) they must apply without distinction to nationals and non-nationals;
  (b) they must be justified by imperative requirements in the general interest;
  (c) they must be suitable for the objective which they pursue; and
  (d) they must not go beyond what is necessary to attain that objective.

- In *Vlassopoulou* [1991], it was held that national authorities must consider any education or training received which is indicated by the qualification and to contrast that with the knowledge and skills required by the domestic qualification. If they are equivalent, then the Member State must recognise the qualification (*see* also *Morgenbesser* [2003]). If they are not considered equivalent, then they must go on to consider the knowledge or training received by the applicant through study or experience, which may be sufficient to make up for what was lacking in the formal qualification. (The decision in this case whereby a Member State is required to carry out a comparative examination of diplomas was incorporated in Directive 99/42 clarifying the rules on the recognition of qualifications).

FREEDOM TO PROVIDE SERVICES

Article 49 deals with the provision of services as set out in Article 50. "Services" under the Treaty are those provided in one Member State for a person in another Member State.

Article 49 provides that:

> "Within the framework of the provisions set out below, restrictions on freedom to provide services within the Community shall be prohibited in respect of nationals of Member States who are established in a state of the Community other than that of the person for whom the services are intended".

Article 50 provides that:

> "Services shall be considered to be 'services' within the meaning of this Treaty where they are normally provided for remuneration, insofar as they are not governed by the provisions relating to freedom of movement for goods, capital and persons. 'Services' shall in particular include:
>
> (a) activities of an industrial character,
> (b) activities of a commercial character,
> (c) activities of craftsmen,
> (d) activities of the professions.
>
> Without prejudice to the provisions of the Chapter relating to the right of establishment, the person providing a service, may, in order to do so, temporarily pursue his activity in the state where the service is provided, under the same conditions as are imposed by that state on its own nationals."

Again the Court has played a major part in clarifying the scope of the Treaty provisions, in particular the prohibition of discriminatory measures by Member States.

In *H.M. Customs & Excise v Schindler* [1994], the Court examined the meaning of "services". Schindler was the agent of state lotteries in Germany who sent letters from the Netherlands to the UK enclosing invitations to play the German lotteries. The Court held that the letters were not goods but services in that they were provided for remuneration and offered in another Member State. However, lotteries and other gaming services can be legitimately restricted on public policy grounds (*see* also *Gambelli* [2003]).

Beneficiaries of both the right of establishment and the freedom to provide services include Community nationals as well as companies formed under the law of one of the Member States. In *Commission v Germany (re Insurance Services)* [1987], the Court held that an enterprise would be regarded as an establishment rather than a provider of services if there was no branch or agency within the Community but only an office managed by an independent person authorised to act on a permanent basis.

Van Binsbergen [1974] concerned the representation in Court of a Dutch national who was not allowed by national rules to have his legal adviser continue to represent him when the legal adviser moved to Belgium. In this case the Court set out the test of necessity and ruled that a residential qualification in a properly qualified person is not a legitimate condition of exercising that profession unless it is necessary to ensure the observance of professional rules of conduct.

In *Gebhard* [1995], the Court gave further guidance on the compatibility of national rules with the Treaty and reiterated the four criteria set out in *Commission v Luxembourg (re Access to the Medical Profession)* [1992], which were considered under freedom of establishment (above). In other words, where national measures restrict one of the Treaty's fundamental freedoms they must be non-discriminatory, be able to be justified in the general interest, be objectively necessary and in proportion to their objective.

In *Bickel and Franz* [1998], an Italian refusal to use the German language in criminal proceedings for non-German speaking Community nationals staying in Italy was unjustified with regard to the objective pursued and would constitute discrimination.

The concept of services also extends to the recipients of services. Although the Treaty makes no express reference to the receipt of services, Directive 73/148 in Article 1(b) sets out that there are to be no restrictions on:

> "(a) nationals of a Member State who are established or who wish to establish themselves in another Member State in order to pursue activities as self-employed persons or who wish to provide services in that state; and
>
> (b) nationals of Member States wishing to go to another Member State as recipients of services."

In *Luisi and Carbone v Ministero del Tesoro* [1984], the Court held that the freedom to provide services includes the freedom for a national of another Member State to receive services under the same conditions as nationals of the host state. The principle of non-discrimination applies (*Cowan v Trésor*

Public [1989]). In the case of medical services, it has been held that UK nationals have the right to receive medical treatment outside the UK, where there has been an inordinate delay in receiving treatment on the NHS and to receive reimbursement of the costs incurred (*Watts* [2006]).

In *Commission v Italy (re Museum Charges)* [2003], Italian legislation on preferential rates for entry to national museums allowed only to Italian nationals and persons aged over 60 or 65 years resident within the area, was ruled as infringing the principles of free movement of services and non-discrimination.

As regards education, in *Gravier v City of Liège* [1985], a French national challenged the Belgian fee for a vocational course as discriminatory and constituting an obstacle to her Community right to vocational education. This was followed in 1988 by *Blaizot* establishing that all courses save those intended to improve the general education of students rather than prepare them for employment, are considered as vocational courses. The entitlement to loans and grants, however, is still only available to workers and their families as "social and tax advantages" under Regulation 1612/68.

At the end of 2006, the Commission finally secured agreement on the new Services Directive, Directive 2006/123. This new law, in particular, requires the Member States to simplify their formalities applicable to access to services and to create a point of single contact, in relation to the formalities surrounding services. Information on services should be made easily available to potential recipients and providers of services. The Directive requires the Member States to bring into force domestic law to give effect to the Directive by December 28, 2009.

---

12. CITIZENSHIP AND THE FREE MOVEMENT OF PERSONS

Since its creation in the Treaty on European Union, the title on Citizenship in Articles 17 to 22 of the EC Treaty now sets out that, "Citizenship of the Union is hereby established. Every person holding the nationality of a Member State shall be a citizen of the Union. Citizenship of the Union shall complement and not replace national citizenship". Further, the Treaty sets out that nationals of the Member States have four specific rights:

- To move freely and reside in the territory of Member States;
- To vote and stand as a candidate in local and European Parliament elections in the Member State of residence (not of nationality);
- To protection, in a non-EU country in which the citizen's own Member State is not represented, by the diplomatic or consular authorities of any other Member State; and
- To petition the European Parliament and to apply to the European Ombudsman and to receive a reply in the citizen's own language.

The wording of the Treaty indicated that no new free movement rights for persons were to be brought into being, but solely attached the existing rights—with all their qualifications and derogations—to the new concept of citizenship. Although the exact rights of citizens were unclear, it was not long before cases arrived before the European Courts in which citizenship was a central issue:

- *Uecker and Jacquet* [1997]—citizenship was not intended to extend the scope of the Treaty to cover internal situations with no link to Community law.
- *Martinez Sala* [1998]—any Spanish national living in Germany not falling within the Community definition of "a worker" (i.e. not carrying out economic activity) and thus not falling within the personal scope of the legal provisions was still entitled to equal treatment in relation to welfare as she came within the material scope of these benefits.
- *Grzelczyk* [2001]—a French student in Belgium again, not a "worker" in the Community sense and thus not entitled to benefits was considered to have been discriminated against contrary to Article 12 of the Treaty in conjunction with the Treaty provisions on citizenship.
- *Baumbast* [2002]—a citizen of the Union who no longer enjoyed a right of residence in a host Member State possessed a fundamental right to move and reside freely within the Union, subject to limitations and conditions laid down elsewhere in Community law. Such limitations must be exercised in accordance with the principle of proportionality, may not be arbitrary nor must they deprive the residence rights endowed of their substantive content.
- *Zhu and Chen* [2004]—A Chinese couple visited the United Kingdom. The wife gave birth to a daughter whilst in Belfast. The child gained Irish nationality and thus EU citizenship. Mrs Chen moved to Cardiff and sought residency for her family, which was denied. The Court of Justice stated that by virtue of Article 18 (and applicable secondary legislation) parents could not be deprived of their right to reside with their child, who is a Union citizen.

With the *Baumbast* case came the recognition by the Court that Article 18 was directly effective and therefore could be relied on to provide rights which an individual could enforce through local courts. However, there was also a need to clarify the exact procedural and substantive rights that Union citizens possess by virtue of their status as Union citizens and as such Directive 2004/38 (The Citizenship Directive) was enacted (discussed above).

13. EQUAL TREATMENT

EQUAL TREATMENT

Equal treatment was not originally mentioned in the Treaty. Rather, the Treaty only considered equal treatment in two specific circumstances, namely the right not to be discriminated against on grounds of nationality, via old Article 6 (now Article 12) and the very specific economic right of equal pay for men and women, to be found in Article 119 (now Article 141) of the Treaty. Now, the Treaty provides for a range of non-discriminatory safeguards and equality provisions. Indeed, non-discrimination is a fundamental general principle of EC law (*Navas* [2006]). Examples include:

- Articles 2 and 3—promotion of equality for men and women through gender mainstreaming.
- Article 12—non-discrimination on grounds of nationality.
- Article 13—an enabling provision, permitting action to combat discrimination on grounds of race, age, disability, religion and sexual orientation.
- Article 34—non-discrimination between producers or consumers.
- Articles 39-50—equal treatment for workers, self-employed persons and service providers.
- Article 86—equality to be observed by public undertakings.
- Article 90—non-discriminatory taxation.
- Article 137—sex equality in the workplace.
- Article 141—equal pay, including equal pay for equal work.
- Equality as a general principle of law—(*Assurances de Credit v Council and Commission* [1991]).

Since the EC Treaty is a framework treaty, the Treaty rights against discrimination and inequality required a raft of secondary legislation to be enacted, in order to fully ensure that these rights were protected throughout the Union.

In terms of equal pay, its original provisions were expanded by the Treaty of Amsterdam though its underlying principles remain the same. It relates to the fundamental principle of equal pay for male and female workers for equal work (or work of equal value). The object in including such provisions was not only as it first appeared, for social reasons but its underlying rationale— since it dealt originally only with pay rather than all discrimination based on sex—was in keeping with the other economic provisions of the Treaty. It would therefore prevent Member States from deriving any competitive advantage over those who already had equal pay legislation, notably France. However, the Court later was to declare that this Article was intended, by common action, to ensure social progress and to seek the constant improvement of working conditions. Consequently, the following directives to elaborate on the basic Treaty principles of equality and non-discrimination have been adopted:

- Equal Pay Directive 75/117;
- Equal Treatment Directive 76/207 (as amended by Directive 2002/73);
- Equal treatment for men and women in matters of social security—Directive 79/7;
- Equal treatment between self-employed men and women and on the protection of self-employed women during pregnancy and motherhood—Directive 86/613;
- Pregnancy and Maternity Directive 92/85;
- Working Time Directive 93/104;
- Framework agreement on parental leave—Directive 96/34;
- Equal Treatment in Occupation Pensions Directive 96/97 (amending Directive 86/378);
- Burden of Proof in Sex Discrimination Cases (if a claimant has established discrimination, it shall be for the employer to prove that there has been no breach of the principle of equal treatment)—Directive 97/80 (amended by Directive 98/52);
- Framework Agreement on part-time work—Directive 97/81;
- Directive 2000/43 on race and ethnic origin;
- Framework Directive (Directive 2000/78 on equal treatment in employment and occupation); and
- Directive 2004/113 on equal treatment of men and women in access to goods and services.

(1) Equal Pay

Article 141 has direct effect—not only vertical in that a Member State is bound by the Treaty provisions towards its citizens, but horizontal so that individuals such as private companies are bound to comply with its provisions in their treatment of employees (*Defrenne v SABENA* [1976]).

The Community has thus endeavoured to give Article 141 as wide a scope as possible. It has extended the concept of "discrimination" to cover not only direct but also indirect discrimination. Indirect discrimination may arise as a result of employment practices which seem to be based on neutral considerations but which in fact have the practical effect of putting one sex at a disadvantage towards the other. This type of discrimination is not necessarily unlawful if it can be proved that it is capable of objective justification (*Rinner-Kuhn* [1989]).

The first two paragraphs of Article 141 state:

"Each Member State shall ensure that the principle of equal pay for male and female workers for equal work or work of equal value is applied.

For the purpose of this Article, 'pay' means the ordinary basic or minimum wage or salary and any other consideration, whether in cash or in kind, which the worker receives directly or indirectly, in respect of his employment, from his employer.

Equal pay without discrimination based on sex means:
(a) that pay for the same work at piece rates shall be calculated on the basis of the same unit of measurement;
(b) that pay for work at time rates shall be the same for the same job."

Notwithstanding the definition within the Treaty, the notion of "pay" raised questions as to the exact scope of the provision. A series of cases has established that "pay" can include:

- Concessionary travel facilities after retirement (*Garland v BREL* [1982]);
- Statutory Sick pay (*Rinner-Kuhn v FWW* [1989]);
- Private occupational pension schemes (*Worringham and Humphries v Lloyds Bank Ltd* [1981] and *Barber v Guardian Royal Exchange* [1990]);
- Indemnities paid under statute to workers attending day-release training courses (*Bötel* [1992]);
- Severance pay negotiated under a collective bargaining agreement (*Kowalski* [1990]); and
- Maternity pay (*Gillespie v Northern Ireland Health and Social Services Board* [1996]).

Directive 75/117 was introduced to clarify the position of workers who, for example, carry out the same work but where one job is paid less than another where lesser skills and qualifications are required; or where a woman is paid less than a man doing a job that, although different, is alleged to be of comparable economic worth. It concerns equal pay for work of equal value. The directive requires Member States to set up methods whereby an evaluation of comparability may be undertaken at the request of an employee. Since the Treaty of Amsterdam this duty is provided for within the text of Article 141 itself (see above).

(2) Equal Treatment
Although equal treatment of men and women was not mentioned in the Treaty, its scope has been extended through a series of directives (see above) seen as a necessary corollary to the Equal Pay Directive. In particular, the Equal Treatment Directive 76/207 elaborates on the principles of equality of access to employment including promotion, to vocational training and as regards working conditions. Many of its provisions have since fallen into the scope of the Pregnancy and Maternity Directive 92/85.

The Equal Treatment Directive also provides for strictly defined derogations from its provisions under certain circumstances. Article 2(2) of the directive, for example allows exemption from the equal treatment principle for activities for which the sex of the worker constitutes a determining factor (*Sirdar* [1999]). In *Kalanke v Freie Hansestadt Bremen* [1995], the Court limited the interpretation of the derogation in Article 2(4) and held that national rules to give automatic priority to female candidates where they were under-represented in the event that male and female candidates for a job were equally qualified, went beyond the bounds of promoting equal opportunity. The scope of the judgment was clarified in *Marschall v Land Nordrhein-Westfalen* [1997] where it was held that providing an objective assessment taking account of all the criteria specific to individual candidates was made, such positive action would be acceptable as long as the criteria themselves did not discriminate against women. The test would be that preference for a woman would be displaced where reasons specific to an individual male candidate tilted the balance in his favour.

The scope for measures in favour of the disadvantaged sex in employment has been extended with the Treaty of Amsterdam. The aim of gender equality is covered in Article 2 and in Article 3(2) of the Treaty (as amended) which sets out, "[i]n all the activities referred to in this Article, the Community shall aim to eliminate inequalities, and to promote equality, between men and women". Article 13 entitles the Commission to take initiative to combat discrimination. In addition, the fourth paragraph of Article 141 now reads:

> "With a view to ensuring full equality in practice between men and women in working life, the principle of equal treatment shall not prevent any Member State from maintaining or adopting measures providing for specific advantages in order to make it easier for the under-represented sex to pursue a vocational activity or to prevent or compensate for disadvantages in professional careers."

The development of equal treatment for men and women was originally restricted to instances of discrimination arising as a consequence of economic activity, that is in the sphere of employment and self-employment. The scope of equal treatment has been extended by Directive 2004/113 to include equal treatment in access to and the supply of goods and services. This directive has proven to be highly controversial, with Member States highlighting such problems as the actuarial differences between the risks posed by male and female drivers respectively

(3) The General Principle of Equal Treatment
As a point of principle, equal treatment cannot be restricted to prohibiting discriminatory treatment on grounds of sex. Thus, the Commission took advantage of the new provision of Article 13 of the EC Treaty to enact the Race Directive 2000/43, the Framework Directive 2000/78 and the Equal Treatment Directive 2002/73. Combined, these provisions outlaw discrimination based on gender, sexual orientation, racial or ethnic origin, religion or belief, disability and age.

The present equal treatment regime of the Community has advanced considerably from its earliest incarnation as an adjunct to the creation of the single market. Human rights conceptions of equality and non-discrimination now influence (progressive) developments in this area more than conceptions based on economic imbalance and unfairness.

---

14. COMPETITION LAW AND POLICY

The tasks of the Community are set out in Article 2 of the Treaty and include the promotion of a "harmonious and balanced and sustainable development of economic activities" alongside the overarching task of creating and ensuring the proper functioning of the internal market. The primary means of achieving this was by dismantling governmental barriers to trade, such as customs duties, discriminatory taxation and quantitative restrictions.

However, whilst recognising that dismantling Member States' barriers against competition from goods from other Member States was necessary to create a Common Market, this would not on its own be sufficient if businesses were allowed to distort the market to their advantage and to the disadvantage of competitors and consumers. Businesses could easily re-erect commercial barriers to trade. Article 3 sets out how the Community's tasks are to be achieved by activities such as creating and maintaining "a system ensuring that competition in the internal market is not distorted" (Article 3(g)). Two fundamental objectives of the Community—market integration and the promotion of competitive markets within the Community itself—are thus incorporated within the Treaty.

The objectives of European competition policy incorporate equality or fairness. The Treaty Articles relating to state aid for example, ensure that Member States do not favour their own national industries by providing monetary or fiscal advantages to them alone and not to competitors from other Member States. Any such subsidies must be compatible with the provisions as set out in the Treaty.

The Community is also a major world trading bloc. Because the size and sophistication of the companies within the Community who are seeking to enter this global market can differ markedly, it is in the Community's interest that economic integration proceeds as speedily and efficiently as possible to bring prosperity to its manufacturing and service industries. Competition policy therefore also seeks to create and maintain a healthy competitive economic base and in particular to encourage the growth of small and medium-sized enterprises (SMEs) which are economically valuable both to their own Member State and to the Community as a whole, as well as encouraging an "enterprise culture" within Europe. Legal certainty within the small-business community is also recognised as essential to a competitive market.

The importance of protecting consumers—whether as retailers acquiring goods for re-sale or users of the end product—from the effects of anti-competitive conduct is also recognised. The Treaty sets out that consumers should receive a fair share of the benefit of any agreements made between businesses. This can range from a greater variety of products, improved service or guaranteed facilities to more retail outlets for the goods in question.

By promoting a healthy competitive culture within Europe and thus encouraging efficient production and effective allocation of goods and services between Member States and as part of a wider market, efficiency is also recognised as being one of the major aims of competition policy. However, Community competition rules are not designed to promote efficiency at all costs. If this were so, it would protect the most efficient companies at all times and eliminate small and less efficient firms from potential new markets. In turn this would have an adverse effect on the objectives of integration, competitiveness and fairness. What the Community is concerned with is the structural behaviour of undertakings in a market and eliminating barriers to entry for new and potential entrants; legal, fiscal, historical and cultural barriers. Thus, the competition rules are concerned with the control of dominance within a market, the methods by which undertakings acquire and hold on to market power and the degree of interaction taking place between firms.

Because competition policy is dynamic, existing within an intensely economic and political environment, it has evolved from minimal provisions in the original EEC Treaty, through the case law of the Court of Justice and the developing institutional awareness of the Commission into a mature and comprehensive system of rules applying throughout an increasing number of industrial and service sectors of the Community's economy.

Thus, European Community competition rules seek to contribute to the promotion of market integration, to the strengthening of consumer protection and to the maximisation of economic performance within Member States. Competition policy is therefore central to the establishment and maintenance of an open market economy, enabling business and industry throughout the European Community to compete effectively and efficiently in the global arena.

The main provisions of the Treaty relating to competition policy are Article 81 which aims to control anti-competitive practices such as agreements which prevent, restrict or distort competition and Article 82 preventing undertakings from abusing a dominant position. Certain forms of anti-competitive conduct may infringe both Articles, since Articles 81 and 82 are not mutually exclusive (*Unilever Bestfoods v Commission* [2006]; *Hoffmann La Roche* [1979]). These two Treaty Articles complement others to control government intervention aimed at sheltering national industries, such as those found in Articles 87 to 89 relating to state aid and Article 86 covering publicly controlled undertakings.

These are supplemented by secondary legislation to reinforce and expand the outline Treaty provisions, notably Regulation 139/2004, the Merger Regulation. This regulation prohibits concentrations between companies which would significantly impede effective competition in the common market or in a substantial part of it, in particular as a result of the creation or strengthening of a dominant position. Concentrations falling within the threshold limits of the regulation must be notified to the Commission for prior approval.

Not only do the competition rules apply to companies operating anti-competitively within Member States but also to parent companies located outside the EU and their European subsidiaries (*Istituto Chemioterapico Italiano SpA and Commercial Solvents Corporation v Commission* [1973]), and to agreements made between non-EC companies if their practices were implemented in the Community (*Ahlström (A) Oy v Commission* [1993]).

Through Directorate-General IV (DGIV) which is responsible for competition policy, the Commission still plays a key role in the enforcement of the Community's rules on competition within the Member States and can instigate proceedings for infringements of competition law. In accordance with Regulation 1/2003, the Commission and the national competition authorities have extensive powers of investigation and enforcement (see below).

Infringement of the competition rules may incur severe financial penalties, particularly in the case where undertakings horizontally co-operate in a cartel. To date, the largest ever fine in respect of a cartel is that imposed on the lift manufacturers Otis, KONE, Schindler and ThyssenKrupp. The cumulative total of the fine was €992 million [IP/07/209]. The Commission is entitled to levy fines of up to 10 per cent of global turnover for the preceding financial year whichever is the greater (including all group turnover), for intentional or negligent infringement of Articles 81 and 82. It may therefore be assumed that the deterrent effect of disregarding the Community's competition rules is considerable. In fixing the amount of the fine, the Commission will have regard both to the gravity and duration of the infringement (*Group Danone v Commission* [2007]; *Commission Notice on immunity from fines and reduction of fines in cartel cases* [2006] OJ C 298/11; *guidelines on the method of setting fines imposed pursuant to Article 23(2)(a) of Regulation 1/2003* [2006] O.J. C 210/02). In addition, private enforcement of competition law by way of damages actions in the national courts is playing an increasingly important role in deterring companies from acting anti-competitively (*Courage v Crehan* [2001]; *Green Paper on Damages actions for breach of the EC antitrust rules* COM (2005) 672).

Article 81 is now directly effective in its entirety (Regulation 1/2003).

ARTICLE 81

Article 81 prohibits collusive behaviour between undertakings which would have an effect on competition and affect trade between Member States. The Article itself is in three parts. Article 81(1) sets out the prohibited conduct, Article 81(2) the consequences of indulging in such anti-competitive behaviour and Article 81(3) allows the Commission, national courts and national competition authorities to exempt agreements under certain conditions. It reads as follows:

"(1) The following shall be prohibited as incompatible with the common market: all agreements between undertakings, decisions by associations of undertakings and concerted practices which may affect trade between Member States and which have as their object or effect the prevention, restriction or distortion of competition within the common market, and in particular those which—
(a) directly or indirectly fix purchase or selling prices of any other trading conditions;
(b) limit or control production, markets, technical development, or investment;
(c) share markets or sources of supply;
(d) apply dissimilar conditions to equivalent transactions with other trading parties, thereby placing them at a competitive disadvantage;
(e) make the conclusion of contracts subject to acceptance by the other parties of supplementary obligations which, by their nature or according to commercial usage, have no connection with the subject of such contracts.
(2) Any agreements or decisions prohibited pursuant to this Article shall be automatically void.
(3) The provisions of paragraph (1) may, however, be declared inapplicable in the case of:
—any agreement or category of agreements between undertakings;

—any decision or category of decisions by associations of undertakings;

—any concerted practice or category of concerted practices,

which contributes to improving the production or distribution of goods or to promoting technical or economic progress, while allowing consumers a fair share of the resulting benefit, and which does not:

(a) impose on the undertakings concerned restrictions which are not indispensable to the attainment of these objectives;

(b) afford such undertakings the possibility of eliminating competition in respect of a substantial part of the products in question.

"Agreement"

The meaning of the term "agreement", within the context of Article 81(1) is wider than simply a contractual obligation, whether written or oral. Even an arrangement between parties that is not legally binding may constitute an agreement (*Re Polypropylene* [1988]), as does a "gentleman's agreement" enforceable by arbitration (*ACF Chemiefarma* [1970]).

Agreements may be "horizontal", that is between companies at the same level of trade or industry (the parties are all manufacturers, distributors, retailers, etc.) or "vertical", between companies at different levels of a trade or industry (a manufacturer with a distributor, a wholesaler with a retailer and so on). Both types of agreement may fall within the prohibitions of Article 81(1) (*Société Technique Minière* [1966]).

Unilateral action taken by a manufacturer to refuse the supply of certain goods to its distributors has also been defined as "an agreement" (*Ford Werke v Commission* [1985]). The Court ruled that this ostensibly one-sided arrangement was so closely connected to a system of individual agreements between the manufacturer and its distributors that the unilateral action was part of the whole contractual framework between the manufacturer and its distributors.

"Undertakings"

In the absence of any precise definition within the Treaty, the Court has interpreted the concept of an undertaking widely to include any economic entity, company, partnership, sole trader or group of companies, whether providing goods or services, commercial or cultural, public or private. Examples of undertakings range from opera singers (*RAI/Unitel* [1978]), to port authorities (*Merci Convenzionale Porto di Genova v Siderurgica Gabrielle SpA* [1991]). The fact that an entity is state-owned or state-financed and provides a service normally provided by the state does not prevent it from being considered an undertaking if it provides services of "general economic interest" (*Job Centre Co-op.* [1998]).

The Court will also regard as one undertaking, companies that are ostensibly legally separate such as parent companies and their subsidiaries but which in fact are linked through ownership and management agreements (*Viho Europe BV v Commission* [1996]). In these cases, the Court applies the "economic entity" principle, judging both companies to be one undertaking when a sufficient degree of control is exercised by the parent to leave no room for independent management by the subsidiary. Agreements made between the two will then be considered as an allocation of functions (*Béguelin* [1971]).

"Decisions by associations of undertakings"

An "association of undertakings" refers to a trade association, federation or syndicate. An example of a prohibited activity would include the recommendation of prices even if such recommended prices were claimed to be non-binding (*Vereeniging van Cementhandelaren v Commission* [1972]), or a non-binding code of conduct (*Publishers' Association v Commission* [1992]).

"Concerted practices"

Where two or more undertakings co-operate—no matter how informally—on some co-ordinated anti-competitive practice, such as price fixing or refusal to supply, such activities may result in investigation under Article 81(1). Even though no formal agreement may exist between the undertakings involved, the Court has nevertheless defined "concerted practice" as:

> "a form of co-ordination between enterprises that has not yet reached the point where it is a contract in the true sense of the word but which, in practice, consciously substitutes practical co-operation for the risks of competition (*ICI v Commission (Dyestuffs)* [1972])".

Although evidence of collusive practices between companies can be difficult to establish, apparently inter-related behaviour such as price rises or other parallel conduct in itself will not necessarily constitute proof of a concerted practice (*Åhlstrom (A) Oy v Commission* [1993]).

In order to determine whether any agreements reached by undertakings fall within the prohibition laid down by Article 81(1) of the Treaty, the Court has regard to three distinct elements:

- Whether the object or effect of the agreement is to restrict competition;
- Whether such restriction applies to an appreciable extent within the common market; and
- Whether the agreement may affect trade between Member States.

"Object or effect"

The Court has ruled that there is no need to take account of the practical effect of an agreement once it appears that it has as its object the prevention, restriction or distortion of competition (*Société Technique Minière* [1966]). However, if the object of an agreement is clearly not anti-competitive, consideration will then be given to its effect (*Delimitis v Henninger Bräu* [1991]). Examination of the agreement within its economic and legal context will then take place to reach a conclusion as to whether the effect of the practice breaches Article 81(1) on the basis of:

- The nature or quantity of the products to which the agreement relates;
- The position and importance of the parties in the relevant product and geographical markets;
- Whether the agreement is isolated or part of a network;

- The severity of the restriction; and
- The existence of patents, trademarks or other intellectual property.

"The prevention, restriction or distortion of competition within the common market"

The list of agreements capable of distorting the structure of the market is set out in Article 81(1) but is by no means exhaustive. The essential element is that collusion between undertakings capable of distorting the structure of the market has taken place. Distortion can also arise through the existence of an agreement between two undertakings and a third, which is not party to the original agreement (*Consten and Grundig v Commission* [1966]).

"To an appreciable extent"

This is known as the *de minimis* doctrine. Even though the wording of the Treaty indicates that any effect on competition and trade between Member States is sufficient to trigger the application of Article 81, the Court confirmed early on that this must be "appreciable" (*Völk v Vervaecke* [1969]). Shortly afterwards, in the early 1970s, the Commission clarified this judgment by publishing a guidance Notice on Agreements of Minor Importance quantifying the *de minimis* threshold. The most recent Notice ([2001] O.J. C368/13) provides that agreements concerning goods or services will not be considered under Article 81(1) if the market share of all the participating undertakings in the relevant markets does not exceed:

- A 10 per cent threshold where the agreement is made between undertakings operating at the same level of production (horizontal agreements); or
- A 15 per cent threshold where the agreement is made between undertakings operating at different levels of production (vertical agreements); and
- Small and medium sized enterprises (SMEs) are considered by the Commission to be rarely capable of appreciably affecting trade between Member States. The Commission considers that agreements between SMEs therefore generally fall outside the scope of Article 81(1).

"Which may affect trade between Member States"

If an agreement is not capable of affecting trade between Member States—actually or potentially—Article 81 will not apply. For the agreement to fall within Article 81, it is sufficient that the agreement is likely to affect trade, even in the future.

If an agreement is made, *the effects of which are confined to the territory of a single Member State*, it does not fall under Article 81, but is governed by the national legal order (*Hugin Cash Registers v Commission* [1979]). In order to assist companies in determining whether their agreement is caught by EC competition law, the Commission issued guidance in 2004 on the effect of trade concept contained in Articles 81 and 82 of the Treaty ([2004] O.J. C 101/81).

Exemptions
Although an agreement has, or is intended to have an anti-competitive effect,
it may be subject to an exemption from the prohibitions in Article 81(1). In
an attempt to balance the economic interests of undertakings, consumers and
the Community itself with the desire to avoid unnecessary restrictions on
business enterprise, Article 81(3) provides for some agreements, decisions or
concerted practices which, although they reduce competition, may also have
beneficial consequences which outweigh their restrictive effects; which
contribute towards improving the production or distribution of goods; or to
promoting technical or economic progress whilst allowing consumers a fair
share in the benefits of such arrangements. As well as possessing these
"positive" attributes, the arrangements made must also abide by two
"negative" conditions. First, they must be no more restrictive than absolutely
necessary in order to achieve the undertaking's apparent objective and
secondly, they must not give the undertakings the opportunity to eliminate
any competitors.

     Until May 2004, the Commission had exclusive jurisdiction to grant
exemptions from the prohibitions laid down in Article 81(1). Since then, the
entire text of Article 81 has been directly effective, that is, the decision as to
whether agreements and decisions satisfy the exemption criteria of Article
81(3) can now be taken by the competition authorities and national courts of
the Member States, in addition to the Commission. The Commission has
therefore lost its monopoly in applying Article 81(3).

Block Exemptions
Under the old centralised system of enforcement of Regulation 17/62, the
Commission was the only body authorised to grant exemptions to the
prohibition of Article 81. For administrative convenience, businesses seeking
the protection of Article 81(3) were required to individually notify their
agreement to the Commission. After investigating the application, the
Commission could prohibit the agreement or, if the agreement was
acceptable, the Commission would issue a comfort letter or grant negative
clearance. Further administrative pressure meant that this system did not
reduce the workload of the Commission to the extent desired. Indeed, the
Commission often faced multiple notifications from businesses in the same
industrial sector. Thus, the Commission resorted to using a general system of
block exemptions, whereby the Commission would issue a prescriptive
regulation for a particular industry sector which outlined the type of
agreements which would satisfy the Commission. Businesses which re-
arranged their operations to fit the rules of the Block Exemption Regulation,
were generally safe from Commission interference.

     In the latter years of its operation, the Block Exemption system came in
for severe criticism. Essentially, the law had a strait-jacket effect, forcing
businesses to conform to a particular model of operation in the marketplace.
This approach stifled development and innovation on the market.
Notwithstanding the criticisms levelled at the Block Exemption system, legal
certainty has required that certain Block Exemption Regulations must remain
valid until their expiry date. In addition, the Commission has continued to
enact Block Exemption Regulations since the new decentralised regime came
into operation. Examples of Block Exemptions in force include:

- Motor Vehicle Vertical Agreements and Concerted Practices (Regulation 2790/99);
- Technology Transfer Agreements (Regulation 772/2004);
- Exclusive Distribution and Purchasing, and Franchising Agreements (Regulation 2790/99);
- Specialisation Agreements (Regulation 2658/2000);
- Research and Development Agreements (Regulation 2659/2000);
- Insurance Agreements (Regulation 358/2003); and
- Air Services and Slot Allocation (Regulation 1459/2006).

In relation to the Block Exemption Regulations which deal with vertical agreements, that is agreement between businesses operating at different levels in the marketplace, it is important to note that acceptance of the benefits of vertical agreements by the Commission, is a relatively recent occurrence. Vertical agreements typically involve a manufacturer and distributor. The benefit of the vertical agreements is that each business is free to concentrate on their particular area of expertise, leaving the other partner to concentrate on their area of expertise. However, vertical agreements have the potential to re-erect national barriers to trade since they typically involve a manufacturer granting geographically limited exclusive or selective distribution rights to a distributor or retailer. Such activities would impede the creation of a fully functioning European Internal Market. Thus, the Commission has been keen to keep a close eye on such arrangements.

ARTICLE 82

Undertakings that find their ability to form anti-competitive agreements curtailed under Article 81 may seek to merge into a single entity to frustrate the competition rules. Article 82 controls companies seeking to evade prohibition by these means. Otherwise, such undertakings would hold such powerful economic positions that they are not only able to dominate the market in which they operate, but could also derive unfair advantages and eliminate competitors. Article 82 is directly effective and prohibits the following:

> "Any abuse by one or more undertakings of a dominant position within the common market or in a substantial part of it shall be prohibited as incompatible with the common market insofar as it may affect trade between Member States. Such abuse may, in particular, consist in:
> (a) directly or indirectly imposing unfair purchase or selling prices or unfair trading conditions;
> (b) limiting production, markets or technical development to the prejudice of consumers;
> (c) applying dissimilar conditions to equivalent transactions with other trading parties, thereby placing them at a competitive disadvantage;
> (d) making the conclusion of contracts subject to acceptance by the other parties of supplementary obligations which, by their nature or according to commercial usage, have no connection with the subject of such contracts."

Unlike Article 81 which deals with agreements between one or more undertakings, Article 82 primarily deals with the abuse of a dominant position by (usually) a single company. Although the prohibited conduct set out in Article 82 closely corresponds to the examples set out within Article 81(1), again, these are not exhaustive. The case law of the Court confirms that the open list of examples provided in the body of Article 82 can be extended.

The prohibition contained in Article 82 is absolute and admits of no exceptions.

Article 82 comes into operation when three factors exist:

- A dominant position is held by one or more undertakings either within the common market or within a substantial part of it;
- That dominant position is abused; and
- The abuse in question affects trade between Member States.

Once again, in the absence of detailed definition within the Treaty, the case law of the Court defines the terms.

"Dominant position"

In order to establish dominance, it must be established that the undertaking in question was dominant in a particular market. This is usually taken to mean that the undertaking concerned "has the power to behave to an appreciable extent independently of its competitors, customers and ultimately of its consumers" (*United Brands v Commission* [1978]; *Microsoft* [2004]).

Relevant Market

The first objective is to define the market in which the undertaking is alleged to be dominant. In other words, it is essential to identify the "relevant market"; what products constitute it and where the geographical boundaries of this market lie.

With regard to the relevant product market, interchangeability of products is the key factor in its identification. If a consumer can easily switch to another item, it would seem that on the face of it, competition within that particular market has not been stifled and there would thus be no necessity for Commission intervention. To assess whether or not interchangeability of products exists, the Commission considers the characteristics of the commodities themselves and those of other goods that can be substituted for them. Products that only have limited interchangeability with others are not usually considered part of the relevant market (*Michelin v Commission* [1983]). From the Commission's point of view, the narrower the definition of the relevant market, the more likely it is that the undertaking will be found to be dominant in that market; while an undertaking would naturally prefer that an assessment would define the market broadly. The test is not set arbitrarily, rather an in-depth economic analysis of the market must be undertaken.

To evaluate the relevant geographical market, the Treaty states that Article 82 will apply to conduct "within the common market or in a substantial part of it". An assessment will look at the level of trading in one or more Member States compared to that in the Union as a whole. It is not necessary for an undertaking to carry out its activities in all Member States of the European Union; even activities in one Member State may be enough to trigger the application of Article 82 provided that these had an effect on trade between Member States (*Michelin v Commission* [1983]).

In order to render its policy and decision making more transparent and thus enable undertakings to enjoy an element of legal certainty when drawing up their agreements, acquisitions and joint ventures, in 1997 the Commission published a Notice setting out guidelines to its definition of the relevant market ([1997] O.J. C372/5).

Establishing Dominance

Once the relevant market has been evaluated, the key objective is to establish dominance of that market. Several factors are relevant to the assessment of an undertaking's dominance.

Two major cases serve to indicate not only the approach of the Commission in establishing anti-competitive conduct under Article 82, but the imprimatur of the Court of their findings. In *Hoffmann La Roche v Commission* in 1979 and *United Brands v Commission* in 1978, the Commission found that dominance would be considered:

- Where large market shares have been in place for a considerable time;
- Where the position of existing and potential competitors is taken into account;
- Where an undertaking's share of the market was appreciably in excess of its competitors;
- Where difficulties were faced by potential competitors trying to break into the market such as instances where customers are locked in to existing products and contracts; and
- Where substantial resources have been expended on product brand image and advertising.

Collective Dominance

Although most incidences of illegal abuse of a dominant position relate to the activities of a single undertaking, Article 82 also condemns anti-competitive conduct by "one or more undertakings". This collective dominance usually takes place when two or more undertakings, because of the economic links between them, hold a collective dominant position on the relevant market (*Società Italiana Vetro SpA v Commission* [1992]). Such a market can often be described as oligopolistic in nature (*Municipality of Almelo v Energiebedrijf Ijsselmij* [1994]).

Abuse

Once it has been established that an undertaking holds a dominant position in a particular market, it is necessary to determine whether or not it has abused this position. Dominance of itself is not illegal. What is prohibited is abuse of the dominant position. The Court has stated that an undertaking in a dominant position "has a special responsibility not to allow its conduct to impair undistorted competition on the common market" (*Michelin v Commission* [1983]). Abuses can be characterised as exploitative [as to the consumer] or exclusionary [as to competitors].

It has condemned abusive practices such as:

- Excessive and discriminatory pricing (*United Brands v Commission* [1978]);

- Predatory pricing (*AKZO Chemie BV v Commission* [1991]; *France Telecom v Commission* [2007]);
- Fidelity rebates (*BPB Industries plc & British Gypsum* [1995] and *Michelin* [2003]);
- Tying-in practices (*Hoffmann La Roche v Commission* [1979]; *Hilti v Commission* [1994] and *Microsoft* [2004]);
- Bundling (Microsoft [2004]);
- Refusals to supply (*Instituto Chemioterapico Italiano SpA* and *Commercial Solvents Corporation v Commission* [1973]) including a refusal to licence intellectual property; *Magill* [1991]).

"Insofar as it may affect trade between Member States"

As with Article 81, if the practice in question does not affect trade between Member States, then Article 82 will not apply. Nevertheless, for the operation of Article 82 to be triggered, it is sufficient that the conduct might affect trade even in the future (*British Leyland v Commission* [1986]).

Enforcement

Directorate-General IV of the Commission (DGIV) plays a significant role in the enforcement of the competition rules, alongside the new powers for national courts and national competition authorities to enforce competition law. Article 85 provides that, "The Commission shall ensure the application of the principles laid down in Articles 81 and 82".

By the early 1990s, it had become clear that effective enforcement of the competition rules was beginning to falter due mainly to the excessive workload placed upon the Commission, notwithstanding the fact that National Competition Authorities were already closely involved in assisting the Commission in enforcing the competition rules. The fact that the majority of Member States had either adopted or amended their own national competition laws to mirror the prohibitions of Articles 81 and 82 and political considerations such as the need to comply with the general principle of subsidiarity of Article 5, which requires decision taking to be made at the closest level to the citizen, resulted in the Commission agreeing to give up its enforcement monopoly.

In September 2000, the Commission published a White Paper on Modernisation of the Rules implementing Articles 81 and 82 within which it set out its proposals for a Council Regulation to reform the rules on competition enforcement particularly in the light of the (then) imminent enlargement of the Union. This new Regulation 1/2003 entered into force in May 2004.

Under Regulation 1/2003, national competition authorities, the national courts and the Commission have the power to apply Articles 81 and 82. In particular, they can require an infringement to be brought to an end, order interim measures, accept commitments and impose fines or periodic penalty payments. National competition authorities are also empowered to apply any other penalty provided for in national law, while the Commission has the power to impose appropriate structural or behavioural remedies to bring the violation to an end. Articles 11 and 15 of the regulation provide for co-operation between the Commission, the national competition authorities and the national courts in applying the European rules. To this end, the Commission has issued a series of non-binding Notices, which provide greater clarity to this co-operative relationship (Notice on Co-operation between the Commission and the national courts [2004] C101/54; Notice on Co-operation within the Network of Competition Authorities [2004] C101/43). The establishment of the European Competition Network has also greatly facilitated co-operation in this area. In addition, the Commission has also promulgated a Notice in 2004 that provided the Commission with the power to issue guidance letters in the case of novel competition law situations ([2004] C101/06). The Commission has also issued a Notice on the application of Article 81(3) of the EC Treaty ([2004] C101/97).

The adoption of a decentralised system of enforcement that involves a wide range of actors across 27 Member States creates the potential risk that inconsistency could creep into decision making, undermining legal certainty and the unity of the European Union competition law system. The adoption of guideline notices as outlined above, coupled with the duty of close mutual co-operation explicit in Regulation 1/2003, has greatly reduced this risk of legal uncertainty.

In order to fully enforce competition law, the Commission has been given wide-ranging investigatory powers, alongside the power to impose penalties on undertakings. The main powers of Regulation 1/2003 are as follows:

Article 18	**Requests for information** Information may be requested from the undertaking, stating the legal basis and the purpose of the request, specifying the information required, setting time-limits and penalties for supplying incorrect or misleading information and indicating the right of appeal to the Court of Justice. A copy is sent to the national competition authority.
Article 19	**Power to take statements** The Commission has power to conduct interviews to collect information. Officials doing so must inform the national competition authority who may accompany Commission officials.
Article 20	**The Commission's powers of inspection** The Commission has power to make "all necessary investigations into undertakings" that is, (1) to enter premises, land and means of transport;

	(2) to examine the books and other business records; (3) to copy and take extracts; (4) to seal the premises for the period necessary for the inspection; (5) to ask for oral explanations and record the answers. After consulting the national competition authority, and with its active assistance, the Commission requires to produce written authorisation specifying the subject matter, purpose of inspection and penalties for incomplete, incorrect or misleading answers, and the right to have the decision reviewed by the Court of Justice. The Member State shall afford necessary assistance requesting assistance of police or other enforcement authority. The national judicial authority shall ensure that coercive measures are proportional and neither arbitrary not excessive.
Chapter VI Article 23	**Penalties** The Commission is entitled to levy fines not exceeding one per cent of the total turnover for any undertaking that intentionally or negligently supplies misleading information, or refuses to comply with decisions requiring production of information. It may impose fines not exceeding 10 per cent of the total turnover.

Article 24	Periodic penalty payments may be imposed not exceeding 5 per cent of the average daily turnover.
Article 27	**Hearings** Before the Commission makes a decision on the merits of a case, it shall give the undertaking concerned the opportunity of being heard on the matters under dispute. The right

	of defence shall be fully respected with access allowed to the Commission's file, subject to legitimate interest of undertakings in the protection of their business secrets.
Article 31	**Review of the Commission's decision** The Court of Justice has unlimited jurisdiction to review decisions whereby the Commission has fixed a fine or periodic penalty payment. It may cancel, reduce or increase the amounts.

Although the Commission was previously under no duty to give advance notification of an investigation to an undertaking (*National Panasonic (UK) Ltd v Commission* [1980]), Article 20(4) of Regulation 1/2003 sets out that the decision of the Commission to inspect an undertaking shall appoint the date on which it is to begin. Moreover, where a compulsory investigation is opposed, an undertaking's rights must also be protected by the procedural guarantees laid down by national law (*Hoechst AG v Commission* [1989]).

Compliance is enforced with the assistance of the "competent authority" in the appropriate Member State. In the UK, this is the Director-General for Fair Trading who can apply for appropriate injunctions to enforce the powers of the Commission. The Commission copies all important papers to the OFT which comments on cases which raise important issues, particularly where UK interests are involved. Its representatives attend hearings in Brussels when companies make their response to the Statement of Objections issued by the Commission and they participate in an Advisory Committee on Restrictive Practices and Dominant Positions which considers decisions before they are made final.

Legal professional privilege may be claimed but not in respect of communications to in-house lawyers or lawyers based outside the Community, essentially on the basis that these categories of lawyer are not sufficiently independent and/or do not possess a sufficiently strong link to the principle of collaborating with the administration of justice. However, the increasing regulation of in-house lawyers is blurring the distinction between in-house and independent lawyers (*Akzo Nobel* [2003]). In any event, the privilege only extends to information closely linked to the subject matter of the investigation (*A M & S Europe Ltd v Commission* [1982]).

Documents acquired by the Commission during the course of its investigations will inevitably be commercially sensitive. The Commission has a general duty not to disclose information on business secrets acquired by it during the course of its investigations (*AKZO Chemie BV v Commission* [1986] and Article 28 of the regulation).

Any information acquired as a result of Commission investigations shall only be used for the purpose of the relevant investigation although national authorities are not precluded from relying on such information when deciding whether or not to initiate national proceedings (*Direcciòn General de Defensa de la Competencia v Asociaciòn Española de Banca Privada* [1992]).

In the event of the Commission finding a breach of the competition rules, an undertaking is not obliged to admit to an infringement and is entitled to refuse to answer questions if its responses would be self-incriminating (*Orkem v Commission* [1989]).

INDEX